The Further Adventures of an Itinerant Consultant

The Further Adventures of an Itinerant Consultant

I hope you like my second book.

With much love

Robin

Robin Voelcker

Contents

Preface

After four years as a management consultant I decided with a friend to branch out on my own. My father had a small consultancy firm that was almost bankrupt so I used this as a vehicle for our venture. We took it into the fields of the Environment and Food Safety. We were helped enormously in our endeavour by legislation that came into force in 1974, The Control of Pollution Act. We knew we were on the right track business wise and at the same time it was gratifying to be returning to my roots. We built up the consultancy and then sold it in 1998 to one of the privatised water companies. Some of the projects we undertook for clients are described in the book, along with the chemistry involved. In some cases client names have been omitted or changed.

I hope you enjoy reading about some of my memorable adventures both at home and around the globe.

1.

Memories of London

One of my first recollections of London is in 1938 when, aged three, my temporary nanny had taken me to Kensington Gardens. It was the time of the Munich crisis and we had gone to the bandstand to listen to soldiers playing patriot tunes. I then lost sight of nanny, panicked and screamed my head off. I looked around but could not see her anywhere. After a few minutes, a middle-aged woman came to see what was wrong. When I explained, this kindly woman took me by the hand and shouted 'Nanny!' as we walked around the bandstand. About a dozen women replied with a 'Yes?'. At that time, just before World War Two, nannies used to congregate in Kensington Gardens, all dressed in grey, with their prams in a row. Ours was referred to as Nanny Voelcker.

In 1938 my brother John was born and my mother took on a nanny who had previously been with the Elphingstone family. During this time she used to go home to see her mother in Guildford and on one occasion a young man became very friendly with her on Waterloo station. It seemed they both took the same train most Friday evenings. The friendship developed to the extent that he suggested they should marry. His name was Norton.

She gave up being a nanny to settle down to married life. After a while he said he was not well off and did she have any savings? She had been able to save some money, which he took off her and then promptly disappeared. She tried to find him but without success. So she then had to go back to being a nanny and that's how she ended up with us. At that time my mother placed an advertisement in The Lady magazine and got a few replies. She took on this particular nanny due to her previous experience.

At the interview my mother asked what she wanted in payment. She said she had been earning 14 shillings (70p) per week with the Elphingstones, but that her mother suggested she should ask for 15 shillings week, to which my mother agreed. She would have a half day off on Wednesdays. Myself and my two brothers liked our nanny immensely and she became part of the family.

All went well until 1944. She had not seen her mother for some time, so she decided to visit her in Guildford. She went to Waterloo station and, as fate would have it, met the elusive Mr Norton again. He pointed out that they were still married, but apologised for his sudden departure five years earlier. He said he had been sworn to silence but now he could tell her that he had been working for MI6, the security service, and had had to be smuggled into France that evening. Now that he was back in London he suggested they should set up house together and by the way did she have any savings?

He produced some material for nanny to make sheets and pillowcases on her Wednesday afternoons off. My mother got suspicious as nanny was using the sewing machine and two drawers in her room were filled with sheets and other goods. The material was off-white and seemed thicker than usual. You could not buy this material in shops as there was strict rationing at the time.

An article in the newspapers appeared, revealing that there had been a burglary at a Weybridge firm that made parachutes and barrage balloons for the war effort. Much raw material had been stolen. Mr Norton was arrested and prosecuted, with a number of other offences being taken into account. He received a long prison sentence and was lucky not to have been hanged.

City at War

I remember a day in March 1939 when I was four years old. A barber cycling to work across Hammersmith Bridge noticed a suitcase lying in the carriageway. He picked it up to place it on the pavement and noticed it was extremely heavy. He became suspicious and threw it over the side into the river. It was an IRA (Irish Republican Army) bomb, which exploded, breaking windows in buildings on both sides of the river.

Later that year, just before the start of the war, I also remember windows of department stores in Kensington High Street – Barkers, Derry & Toms and Pontings – being smashed by another IRA bomb.

Once the war started, food, drink, household goods and clothes were rationed. My mother employed a Miss Thompson to carry out repairs, mainly on clothing. Miss Thompson was very short of money and having this work would enable her to add a little to the small amount she had. I was aged about six and I always looked forward to her visits. I was fascinated by the way she carried out repairs and she, in turn, was pleased in my interest. I suspected that she liked having company and listening to my chatter.

On one occasion my mother came to see how she was getting on. I was there at the time and I said, 'I think Miss Thompson is a very pretty lady.' My mother was furious and said to me after she had left, 'You do not talk to staff like that!'

Capital Travel

I took a keen interest in travelling around London on double-decker trams. I was always surprised that some of them did not need overhead wires to pick up the current, unlike trams in other places, which took their current from the running track.

I also enjoyed travelling on London's underground, particular the sub-surface trains on the District and Circle lines (then called the inner circle). They had sliding doors that were not automatic. In the hot weather it was pleasant to travel with the doors open. I never heard of anyone ever falling out.

My regular bus was the number 9 and I will never forget one particular bus conductor on this route. The number 9 stopped outside the Albert Hall and in those days conductors called out the names of the stops. Each time we stopped there he would call, 'Albert Hall, no relation to Henry'. (Henry Hall was the well-known leader of the BBC Dance Orchestra.)

When my brother John and I got the bus I would ask for a full ticket and one for a minor. The conductor would say, 'Who's the half?' At that time John was taller than me even though he was younger. I was very self-conscious about it as my mother kept remarking on it. Her three brothers were 6ft 3in, 6ft 5in and 6ft 6in tall. My father was also was 6ft 3in and I felt I had let the side down. When I was older I grew to the same height as my father, while my brother John ended up at 5ft 9in tall, so all criticism of me stopped.

Trolley Bus

I always liked taking the tram along the Thames embankment, which went in the Kingsway tunnel under Waterloo Bridge surfacing in Kingsway itself. On some routes in London, the trams took power from an overhead cable. An arm had to be unhooked from the top of a tram and the tram conductor had to place the arm on to the cable. The arm taking power from the third rail had to be released and taken on board until needed. We also had trolley buses which were powered by electricity from two parallel overhead cables. They ran on roads like a normal bus. From time to time the arm could become detached and the conductor had the job of replacing it.

In 1938, after the Munich crisis, war looked inevitable. My father arranged for us three boys to stay in Guildford at the house of his friend and he hired a Green

Line single decker to take us there, along with our nanny. The bus was loaded with everything we would need, including our clothes, toys and my younger brother's cot. For me it was a great adventure. Unfortunately, as we neared Guildford my elder brother David felt ill. I remember him sitting on the steps of the bus with the door open, being sick.

Green line

2.

Our German Friends

In 1938 after the Munich crisis, many Jewish families became worried by the way things were unfolding in Germany. First of all there was Kristallnaght, when mainly Jewish businesses had their windows broken and goods looted by Nazi youths. Others had the Star of David daubed on their premises to make further trading impossible. Many of the better-off had their houses attacked and the premises ransacked by drunken Nazi youths. Anything breakable was smashed and houses set on fire. It was impossible for families with children to continue living under these conditions.

Jews who could afford to do so made plans to leave Germany, the majority coming to Britain and the USA. Those with money could change deutsch marks into sterling or dollars up to the beginning of 1938 as a means of exporting their capital. Many had already obtained German passports in expectation of trouble to come. Their exit route was via Denmark or the Low Countries – Belgium, the Netherlands and Luxemburg. Many bribes were necessary to pass through these countries. Even when passage was negotiated successfully, those heading for Britain still had to find a ferry to take them to a British port.

One such family were the Schmeidlers: Carl and Lottie and their three children. Carl had been working for the Krupp Group, which was producing steel. He was a

Looted and Destroyed Synagogue

trained chemist with management experience. Carl needed to get a job and hoped to obtain British citizenship. He contacted the Royal Institute of Chemistry (RIC). His chemical qualification was equivalent to ours in Britain. The RIC contacted my father to see if he could help.

Olympic Games Stamps 1936

My father was running an Analytical and Consulting Chemistry practice, which was started by his grandfather in 1863 under the name of Dr Augustus Voelcker and Sons. My great-grandfather Augustus had come to Britain from Frankfurt in 1850 in his 20s to work with the Professor of Chemistry at Edinburgh University. He had been recommended by Justus von Liebig, probably the leading agricultural chemist in Europe, as being a suitable candidate. Liebig was also a businessman and set up in London Liebig's Extract of Meat Company to make meat extract and corned beef.

After a short stay in Edinburgh, Augustus Voelcker was headhunted by The Royal Agricultural College in Cirencester to be their first Professor of Agricultural Chemistry.

My father said that his firm did not have any vacancies. However, he said he would ask a client to see if they could help Carl Schmeidler. The firm was the Camden Chemical Company. The client company said that the only vacancy they had was in their laboratory. He was interviewed by the company's managing director, who said they would let him know if something more suitable came along.

Carl asked if he could take the analyst's job as he needed the money. So he was taken on at a low salary. Although he had not done a laboratory job for a long time, he was fast and accurate, prepared to work long hours and proved he know his chemistry. He rented accommodation in Camden near the firm's premises.

When Carl said he would like to meet my father, my parents invited him and his wife Lottie to dinner. Fortunately they got on well and compared their German roots. My father said he would help him and his family to gain British citizenship, which he did.

Carl was soon promoted in the firm to middle management, which enabled him to buy a house and send his three children to private schools. His elder son, Gunter, was accepted by London University to study Chemistry and after three years there he obtained a first-class degree. Carl was eventually made a director of the firm and after a few successful years he was able to buy the company.

Every year Carl would take his staff, wives and children to a pantomime. He also included John, my younger brother and me, which was very kind of him. He booked a whole row in the circle. I was pleased my father was not included in these excursions. When we went to the theatre as a family, he managed to embarrass us all by commenting in his loud voice about what was happening on the stage. We went as a family to see the musical South Pacific. In the scene where the French planter is making love to Ensign Nellie Forbush, my father boomed in his loud voice, 'I hope he has not been eating onions.' This produced laughter, or annoyance, to people nearby.

Carl was a keen stamp collector and he brought with him his collection of German stamps up to the time he left Germany. He gave these to my father and then, in 1943, my father gave these to me as I was just starting to collect stamps. One was the issue commemorating the Olympic Games of 1936.

Carl also gave my parents two solid silver candle sticks in the form of Corinthian columns.

In the 1960s a few mini-mills were set up to produce steel from scrapped cars, washing machines and fridges. This is now common practice, but then steel was produced on a large scale from iron ore, which was not economical on a small scale. Carl was responsible for starting a mini-mill in Kent, which was very profitable. What pleased him most was that he was returning to his roots, making steel.

While Carl and his family made a good life in the UK, Carl's brother Josef returned to Germany after the war. He was not a scientist but a salesman. Sadly, he was killed in a plane crash in Southern Germany in 1948. I never met him

3.

High Society

At the age of 18, being at Imperial College and living in London, I thought it was time to meet people of my own age. However, I did not know how to start. Though tall and reasonable in looks, I was shy and unsure of myself. I spoke to my godfather who said his wife had an Irish friend who could probably help. It was arranged for me to meet her.

When we met for tea, it transpired that the Irish woman had a daughter who was doing 'The Season'. This consisted of being presented at Court, ie meeting the Queen, and then attending Queen Charlotte's Ball at Grosvenor House.

The Ball was founded in 1780 by George III to celebrate the birthday of his wife Queen Charlotte. In later years it was used to raise funds for the Queen Charlotte Hospital. When the monarch stopped attending the ball, the girls were obliged to curtsey instead to a large birthday cake.

To be presented, the girl would have to be sponsored by some woman, not necessary a blood relation, who had been presented in the past, and was therefore on the Lord Chamberlain's list of suitable people deemed worthy of being presented to Her Majesty. You also had to be on the Lord Chamberlain's appropriate list in order to be invited to the Royal Enclosure at Royal Ascot and the Royal Garden Party at Buckingham Palace.

There were some women who did not qualify but were keen for their daughter to be presented. On the face of it, this could not happen. However there was a way to achieve this – if you had the cash. Every day there were advertisements in The Times newspaper from women who were on the list, offering their services to those who wanted to get on it. For the sum of £1,000, they would arrange everything, even coaching in etiquette. The guys used to try and spot those girls whose mother had paid the money and which, it was presumed, was probably 'new' money. I remember one girl whose surname was the same as that of a travelling circus that had set up their tent on Clapham Common. The poor girl was asked by one rather snobbish guy, 'Are your people circus folk?'

This event for daughters was strictly in the control of the mothers. Once the young ladies, who all had to be dressed in white, had curtseyed, the dancing started. This was the moment for mothers to look around at the young men who had been brought along to partner debutantes. If she saw a

suitable candidate, she would find out his name and write it in her little book. Mothers often complained that they could not find enough suitable young men. Many would meet after the ball to exchange names and information about the young men. They had a code between themselves and the one I remember best was NST: Not Safe In Taxis.

A mother had to be careful, for not all young men were as they seemed. There was one very friendly character who appeared to be very well off and was very popular. At the end of the season he was arrested. It turned out that, far from being a wealthy catch, he was a crook.

There was an embargo at the time on supplying strategic materials to the Soviet Union. This young man decided to obtain and sell copper, which was on the banned list, to the Russians. In this way he amassed a large sum of money, which enabled him to live far above his means. He was jailed for several years.

Some time later, having been released from prison and adopting a double-barrelled name, he applied to join a club of which I was a member. I thought it was my duty to get him black-balled. I thought about for a while and then another member beat me to it.

I realised that to become part of this world I had to be suitably dressed. This meant acquiring an evening tailcoat and trousers, white waistcoat, white stiff shirt and collars, and white tie. I always wore a red carnation with this outfit. A few guys turned up wearing dinner jackets, which was much frowned upon.

After the girls had 'come out', their parents would arrange rather lavish cocktail parties and balls as a way of searching out a suitable partner. As well as top London hotels, other popular venues for these husband-hunting events included the Belgian Embassy in Belgrave Square, Pall Mall clubs and the Hurlingham Club in Fulham. Some mothers tried to out-do the rest by including a celebrity cabaret. I went to one at Wentworth Golf Club, where Cliff Richard and the Shadows had been recruited. During one interval, I went to talk to Hank Marvin and Bruce Welch (Cliff was having a breather).

At the next party I went to, the hostess had recruited Sammy Davis Junior to provide the cabaret. He liked his visits to Britain since he could stay in the best hotels. In his own country, he was banned from staying in the top hotels because he was black and Jewish. When performing in Las Vegas there was no hotel in the centre that would allow him to stay, though he was allowed to perform in them.

There were also weekend house parties with people who had substantial country houses. I received invitations from people I did not know to spend a weekend with them. This was because I was on the 'list' of suitable young men. There would be up to 12 people invited. There was usually a request that I give another guest a lift down in my car. Not everybody had a car in those days. I enjoyed these parties more than the London ones as I met young people I had never met before.

At that time, the Stock Market was buoyant and money could be made easily by shrewd investing. In those days there was no tax to pay on short-term gains. Hence it was easy for a father to pay roughly £1,000 to fund their daughter's coming-out costs.

I remember going to a party given for twin sisters on a riverboat moored close to the Chelsea Flower Show. The Duke of Kent was among the guests. The boat was not large enough to accommodate everyone and many people, including me, got off the boat to continue the party on the pontoon. Some idiot decided to cast off the mooring line so that the boat floated with the tide downstream and was heading for the upright of a bridge. Fortunately there were two members of the crew on board, who were livid, and who were able to bring the boat back to the pontoon.

At that point the press arrived, followed by the police. Someone on the pontoon decided to turn on a fire hydrant, soaking the journalists. At that point I decided to leave rather quickly as arrests were being made.

Next day there were questions asked in the House of Commons about the behaviour of members of the smart set, who were behaving like idiots, risking life and limb. As one member commented, if they had been teddy boys they would have been prosecuted and fined.

Myself   John

The night before the party, my fellow students at Imperial College reminded me that there was a drinks party in the student's union that evening. I said I would not be going as I was already going out to a party on a boat moored near the Chelsea Flower Show. Next morning the story was front page news in the tabloids. My cover was blown. My fellow students all knew exactly where I had been the night before – socialising with the Nobs. I never lived it down.

On another occasion I was invited to a luncheon party at The River Room of the Savoy Hotel. The River Room overlooks the Thames and can be divided into two smaller rooms or left as one large one. I went into the first room and my name was announced by a footman. The hostess shook me by the hand and said, 'How nice to see you again, it is kind of you to come.' I looked at her and did not recognise her at all. In fact, we had never met before.

Apart from being announced on entry, no one spoke to me. I tried introducing myself to some other guests and was ignored. I thought I would leave, so I went to the Gentlemen's on my way out. There was a very pleasant attendant who greeted me and I told him I was leaving as I had found it very boring.

He said, 'Go back to the party and fetch a bottle of champagne and two glasses.' I did this and we had a long conversation. He was very interesting and told me where in Europe he had worked and all about the people he had met. 'Sir Lawrence Olivier was in here last week, what an interesting man,' was one such snippet. We were then joined by two more guests who also found the party boring. They went back and returned with another bottle of champagne and more glasses. This in part made up for an extremely boring party.

During that time, apart from parties of the kind mentioned above, there were events that one was also expected to attend. These included the Chelsea Flower Show, Royal Ascot and Wimbledon. So my social life was pretty hectic.

I always wrote and thanked a hostess for her party. This kept my name alive on the list and paid off because I was swamped with invitations. I limited myself to two parties a week. My father joked that the Post Office was forced to lay on more postmen to cope with my mail. This, however, worked to my detriment in one respect. My studying at Imperial College suffered, resulting in me only getting a second-class degree.

The 'Season' lasted from tea parties in April and finished after Goodwood at the end of July. It was said that many girls felt they went from Debutante to Debris after the Season was over. The young men were back chasing the new crop of debutantes the following season. After Goodwood many debutantes were taken abroad by their parents to recover.

In the October following my first Season, my brother John and I decided that we would give a party in my parent's South Kensington flat to repay the hospitality we had received. We arranged for a firm to make the floor suitable for dancing. Loose boards had to be firmly attached, then a machine shaved off the top of the boards, followed by a sanding machine.

During the Season the most popular band had been Tommy Kinsman's, so we hired his pianist and percussionist to provide the music. I am glad to say the evening was a great success.

We were rather afraid that Mrs Gilbert-Lodge, aged 84, who lived in the flat below, would object. So we sent her an invitation and to our surprise she accepted. She turned up in full evening dress and thoroughly enjoyed herself. She was an Australian who had lived in UK for many years. Back home, her late husband had run a successful engineering firm which had been shortlisted to build the Sydney Harbour Bridge. However, the contract was awarded to the British firm of bridge builders, Dorman Long and Partners. Mrs Gilbert-Lodge turned out to be an excellent dancer and many of men of my age wanted to dance with her. She said she had not enjoyed herself so much for a long time.

The Cote d'Azur

When I was 19 and my younger brother John was 17 we kept on hearing from friends that their parents were taking them on holiday abroad to the Mediterranean. 'There is quite enough to see in one's own country and no need to go abroad,' said my father. John and I did not agree. We decided to go to the South of France on our own. A friend of my mother's suggested that we should go to Antibes which was cheaper than Nice or Cannes. We decided to take her advice and booked in to the hotel she had suggested. We booked flights on British European Airways (BEA), which was then covering Europe and was separate from British Overseas Airways Corporation (BOAC), which covered the rest of the world.

The Royal Hotel

We flew from Northolt in a Viking plane to La Var airport in Nice. We stayed on the Antibes seafront in the Royal Hotel. It was small but comfortable, with a pleasant covered patio on the ground floor. The food was very good, our French not so good. One day we were shown the speciality of the house, but I did not understand what our waitress said. She explained, 'It is what you call in English, "Vol Au Vent"'. The local red wine was very drinkable.

One evening, a middle-aged woman in the hotel explained that she had been invited to a party being given by a friend on Cap d'Antibes and she asked if we would we like to come along. The party was being given by a retired British Admiral who lived locally.

Admiral Claude Comberlage had enjoyed a most remarkable career in the Royal Navy and the Royal Australian Navy. He was born in 1877 and trained on the Britannia sailing ship, and then at the age of 12 joined the Royal Naval College at Dartmouth. He served as a midshipman in destroyers, cruisers and two battleships, reaching the rank of Commander at the age of 34 and Captain at 38. He was promoted to Rear Admiral on retirement in 1922. During his life he met the Czar of Russia, the Dalai Lama, European royalty, General de Gaulle and many famous people including Noel Coward. He was a strict disciplinarian who played by the book, which could make him unpopular with his crew. He tried living in different parts of the world but decided that Antibes was the place for him and his family, so he built a house there. It was a most enjoyable party.

Picasso Museum on the Point

We had high hopes of meeting my mother's cousin while we out there. Henry Lyon, who spoke excellent French and Italian, had decided to buy a house in Menton called Villa Victoria. He saw himself as an author and despite not appearing to make any money, seemed to be happy. We asked a number of people if they knew where we could find Villa Victoria and weren't having much luck. Fortunately one woman we asked said, 'Do you mean Henry Lyon?' She then drove us to his villa where he lived with his partner.

As well as visiting Menton, John and I went to all the other tourist things, Villefranche, Monaco, Monte Carlo, the Palace, the Casino. We also went to the Picasso Museum in Antibes. Whilst I am not a fan of his Cubic period, his earlier work showed that he was a talented painter. It was, however, interesting to see the transition from a traditional painter to his later works.

An Airspeed Ambassador

Planes and Boats

After two weeks it was time to return home. We flew back to London in a twin-engine plane called an Airspeed Ambassador. This had been designed as a replacement for the ageing Douglas DC3 Dakota. It could carry 60 passengers with a crew of five.

I could not think why but I felt unsafe all the way home. I had a window seat and, it being a high-winged plane, I could see the starboard engine. To my untrained eye it looked as if was overheating. It was a great relief to arrive safely in London. I pointed this out to one of the crew. He said it was only an oil leak, which could often happen. A few weeks later an Ambassador plane crashed on take-off from Munich Airport, killing half the Manchester United Football team, the Busby Babes.

Some time later I was carrying out a consulting assignment in Newcastle. I flew in a BKS airline Ambassador. BKS was a local airline providing the Newcastle to London link. It was founded in 1953 and was in competition with BEA. Its service was not as frequent as BEA's and the planes were slower, but it was cheaper.

Once we had landed, the pilot said there was an emergency and we should leave the plane immediately. Passengers were in no hurry and had started taking hand luggage down from the overhead racks. It was only when the pilot said, 'Get out of this f***ing plane now!' that we suddenly realised this was a real emergency.

A BKS Ambassador plane, which had been downgraded to freight, was coming down fast as its steering mechanism had failed. It could only turn one way. Trying to land it took the tails off two parked Viscount planes and narrowly missed ours. The Ambassador plane crashed next to us, killing all crew and the three racehorses it was carrying. Two grooms survived. It was not a pleasant sight. All other Ambassadors planes were then grounded and later scrapped. The two Viscounts were repaired and fitted with new tailplanes.

In my managing consulting days I used aircraft on a regular basis. The peak was in September 1965 when I did over 20 flights in that month. Apart from the incident mentioned above, every other one was plain sailing.

I went to the South of France again in 1990 as a guest of a well-heeled friend who owned a cruising yacht based in Antibes. This time I travelled by train, taking a taxi from the station to the mooring. There were four of us in the party and a crew of three. We travelled east along the length of the coast and into Italy.

What amazed me was that our host was not interested in seeing ports along the route, but spent the time on his phone to his stockbroker buying and selling stock. I asked him whether the boat had a bow thruster to made parking easier. A bow thruster is a propeller in the bow facing sideways, which allows you to park into small places. They enable larger ships to park without assistance from a tug. Our host did not know what I meant.

He had no idea how to sail the boat. I noticed he left all the sailing to the captain. His main interest apart from shares was studying the yachting magazine, looking at boats for sale. He wanted a larger boat. There was boat sale in Monte Carlo and he and the Captain intended looking at what was on offer.

But when we got to Monte Carlo there were no moorings available. If there had been, the cost would have been many thousands of pounds per night. We had to sail back to Villefranche and anchor there at a price in hundreds rather than thousands of pounds per night. We then took the train back to Monte Carlo. The double decker trains were not easy to get off, having a rather high step. A lady in our party had difficulty alighting. The conductor was a bad-tempered French man who started shouting at us, 'Allez allez! Vite, vite!' We answered by calling him 'Cochon.' My host did not get the boat he wanted: it went at a higher price than he was prepared to pay.

As well as travelling along the coast, we spent an interesting time going inland to see some of the villages. On our last evening our host took us to his favourite restaurant called 'The African Queen', which was also frequented by many a famous face, including David Niven. It turned out to be one of the best evenings on the whole trip.

4.

University Days

Cambridge University

Pembroke College

M y first encounter with The Royal Albert Hall was when I was a student in London. One of the two great halls in London, the Hall is situated between Kensington Gardens and the north part of South Kensington. Originally there was also the Queen's Hall near the BBC in north Regent Street, home of celebrated London Proms conductor Henry Wood. It was destroyed by bombing in World War Two.

The Albert Hall survived the war but did sustain some damage. Repaired and eventually reopened, it took over the role of hosting the Proms. As a venue able to cater for up to 5,000 people, it also catered for many different types of events, including music of all descriptions, boxing, wrestling, tennis, the Chelsea Arts Club new year's party and the Festival of Remembrance.

It was 1955 and I was an undergraduate at Imperial College. The college's union building, just south of the Hall, was publicising a performance by Liberace. As well as being an excellent pianist, the American performer was well known as a flamboyant, effeminate showman, who always had a candelabra on his piano, wore outrageous clothes and flashy rings on most fingers. To our minds, he also had a very 'gay' way of talking.

Beit Building

After much drinking in the union's bar, a number of us decided to stand outside the artist's door to the auditorium. When we arrived, there was already a small crowd of middle-aged women waiting to greet him with calls of, 'We love you Lee.' We drunken students countered this with calls of, 'Go home poofter' and 'We do not want queers here.'

It all became rather heated and the police were called. They threatened to arrest us all if we did not leave. Liberace eventually left by a different exit and in a police van, thankfully thwarting our ill-considered, inebriated plan to remove his trousers in order to determine what gender he really was.

In 1957, I returned to the Hall under more impressive circumstances. Having obtained a degree in Chemistry, I was invited to attend a graduation ceremony there, along with the rest of my year. We were to receive our certificates from the Queen Mother, who was then Chancellor of London University (of which Imperial College used to be a part, now it's a university in its own right). We were told that, upon presentation of our certificate, we should not talk to the Chancellor or shake her hand, we should bow and then move on. I knew the Queen Mother had had a relative at my old public school, so I decided to wear my old Wellington College tie. It didn't go unnoticed. 'Oh Wellington,' she said, as I bowed to her. 'Yes Ma'am,' I replied.

Queen Mother opening the new department

I had another occasion to visit the Hall when my mother's cousin, who owned a box there, asked if myself and my two brothers would like to attend a performance of our choice. He thought it was time for us to experience good music, or some other uplifting activity. We were agreed in our decision: we all wanted to see wrestling. He was very disappointed in our choice and we were never asked again. However, we had a good evening.

Cambridge

Having obtained my Chemistry degree, I then spent a year at Cambridge as a postgraduate student. The difference between the two universities was amazing. At Imperial it was hard work throughout the three years I spent there. At Cambridge it was far more relaxed and there was time to pursue other activities. It brought home to me the difference between a university in the true sense and a technical college.

In recent years a spate of new universities have sprung up. Many of these have been technical colleges, which have been upgraded to university status and offer the same subjects as before. The more go-ahead ones have widened the subjects they provide. To me, a university is a place where you mix with all walks of life, people who have shown that they can flourish in their chosen subject or subjects. Much of the benefit comes from mixing with other intelligent people.

When I went to Cambridge in 1957, about one third came from public and grammar schools, one third from state schools and one third from overseas and military services. In those days students from Oxford, Trinity College Dublin and Cape Town could spend their last year at Cambridge and vice versa. I had two friends I met at Cambridge with whom I kept up during my time working in South Africa.

Austin A7 on top of the Senate House

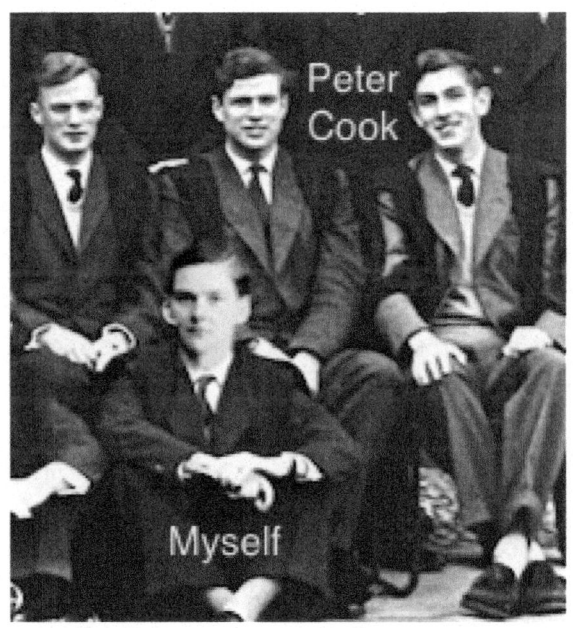

Peter Cook & Myself

While I was studying at Cambridge, there were army students there who were studying engineering. Just before I came down, I was told that someone had placed an Austin 7 car on the roof of the Senate House. The car had been stripped of everything heavy, although it still looked a proper car. I had a look, took a photo and then joined the crowd looking at it. I thought it was a tremendous achievement. It took the authorities about five days to remove it, eventually cutting it up.

In the October of 1957, the freshmen who had just joined the college were assembled outside the Old Reader for a group photograph. Peter Cook, who later became a famous actor and comedian, joined at the same time as me. We became firm friends.

Once I left Cambridge I would return there to enjoy the annual Matthew Wren lunch. Matthew Wren was the uncle of Sir Christopher Wren who, apart from designing Saint Paul's Cathedral and many churches in the City of London, also designed and paid for Pembroke's delightful chapel. He died in 1667 at the age of 81.

The Matthew Wren Society was set up in 1997 for the college to thank members for pledging to help the college financially. The Society has a badge for members to wear in the form of a wren. An annual lunch is held in October of each year and members can bring a guest. An excellent meal and drinks are provided to thank benefactors for their generosity in pledging money.

During one visit to Cambridge to see a client, I decapitated an unsuspecting gnome. I was staying at The Garden House Hotel and was reversing into a space in the carpark when my car came to a stop as I hit something solid. I got out and saw I had struck a stone gnome, breaking it in half. I moved my car about two feet forward, picked up the torso and placed it back on its legs. When I went to drive off, I noticed that the feet were facing backwards. So I got out again and turned the torso to face backwards, then drove off at speed. Hopefully no one noticed.

Mathew Wren Lunch

5.

A Natural Problem Solver

There reached a point when I was having doubts about whether I wanted to continue being a scientist. I was keen to learn more about management and office routines, so I decided to study a course of office management at an evening school in Bishopsgate in the City of London. The course, aimed at people who want to become company secretaries, included Economics, Mercantile Law and Company Accounts.

A friend of mine, Flavia Pelham Burn, suggested I talk to her father who worked for PA Management Consultants. He suggested that I booked an interview with Vocational Guidance to steer me in the right career direction. It was an American idea, but proving useful in the UK as well.

I started by having an interview with one of their consultants. You spend all morning answering about 3,000 trivial questions. I was careful not to tell the consultant too much as I did not want him to sell me back my own ideas. The results were fed into a computer to draw graphs of my aptitude, ability and personality. It would also identify any inconsistencies in my answers.

The principal conclusions were that my attitude towards my fellow beings was low and that I should not consider going into the church, local government or the medical profession. A further recommendation was that, since music was important to me, I should take up an instrument if I did not already play. I did, in fact, play the piano. It was also suggested that, with my background in chemistry, I had an analytical approach to problem solving, so management consultancy, work study or finance should be considered.

I approached a management consultancy called P-E Consultants Ltd and was interviewed. They said they did not have any immediate vacancies but would take me on as a temporary consultant. An experienced consultant was running the assignment and he needed help.

I was sent to work at the premises of a firm in Pentonville Road, near Kings Cross Station, called Stedall Industrial Products. It was a long-established firm that sold parts for the motor industry and architectural ironmongery, but it was no longer profitable. They had a large building, which mainly contained parts for the motor industry, many being redundant stock.

The office staff had a relaxed way of working when someone called about items they required. The stock answer office was, 'He is out at the moment', or 'He will call you back'. This he rarely did.

The office was managed by a man called Baldwin and everyone called him Stanley. On one occasion he used his stock answer to explain non-delivery of items ordered, namely the bad service and incompetence provided by the Post Office. 'What's the name of your company?' he asked the disgruntled caller. 'Oh, you are the Post Office.'

The company had received an offer from a larger group and our job was to see what it would take to make it profitable. We were faced with the task of listing the stock. They had a rather old card-index system which had not been kept up to date. It had, however, been useful in telling what items were stocked. We needed assistance with this task and asked for help from the local labour exchange. The people interviewed were largely not suitable for the job, which required hard work and accuracy. One candidate, however, seemed ideal and we took her on. Her previous job was with

Ivy Benson's Ladies Dance Band. Dance Bands had been very popular from the 1940s to 1960s, but tastes had changed and they could no longer survive.

We discovered that much of the stock were non-movers or valueless and could be sold off. We were able to suggest that, if they concentrated on popular lines and thereby reduced their stock, they would not need such a large building and could move to smaller premises.

At the end of the assignment my senior consultant said he was pleased with the work I had done. The firm was expanding at the time and it was recommended that I be taken on by P-E and sent for training at their centre in Egham. There were 10 people on the intake for training and the firm had booked us into a small hotel in Old Windsor. On arrival we checked in and then went to have an evening meal in the dining room.

To accommodate the whole group, we moved two tables together to make one large one where we could all sit. The proprietor lost her temper when she saw our rearrangement of the furniture and threw us out of the hotel. I had visions of us having to spend the night in our cars. We thought we would try the Lodge Hotel in Englefield Green. Thomas, one of our number, said he had stayed in the hotel with his parents when he was younger.

Miss Hilda Downie, the owner, said she had had trouble with trainees from P-E in the past and had decided therefore not to take any more in future. Thomas saved the day by talking to Miss Downie, who remembered him. We were then allowed in. Crisis averted, we started training the following day.

6.

The Novelty of TV

I n 1944 our family stayed in a village called Meppershall in Bedfordshire. It was a time when V1s and V2s were raining down on London and the home counties. The owner of the house had been general manager of HMV, the gramophone company in Hayes. Not surprisingly, he was keen on music and had a collection of about 5,000 78rpm records. He also had one of the first televisions in the country.

This was a complete novelty for me. Not having seen one before, I was fascinated by it. Television programmes had been discontinued in 1939 at the outbreak of war and started up again in 1947. They were broadcast from Alexandra Palace in North London.

The first programmes after the war were those shown before the shutdown. There was much singing and dancing, some of which were screened live from west-end theatres. To me, the new programmes made after the war were not as good as those made before. They were very formal, with male announcers always dressed in dinner jackets. I will always remember announcer MacDonald Hobley introducing the Chancellor of the Exchequer as Sir Stifford Craps instead of Sir Stafford Crips.

There was only BBC in those days, so there was no competition. Many old

American films were shown. Some parlour games, such as What's My Line, This is Your Life and Twenty Questions, were imported from the USA but with British personnel.

My interest in radio and TV started properly when I was at boarding prep school in 1945 and saw a boy making a crystal radio set. It did not need batteries, just an aerial and earth connection. I thought I should investigate. I bought a magazine called Practical Radio regularly and quickly learned how to construct radios with valves instead of crystal sets. My mother could not find a radio small enough for her bedside table, so I made her one. I also made a few for other people.

I still had in the back of my mind the TV set I had seen in 1944. Sales of black and white TVs took off with the Queen's Coronation in 1953. My father made it plain that he would not have a TV in our home at any cost. About this time, my father was approached by a well-known entrepreneur, Graham Farish, for help in producing a plant fertiliser in tablet form. A well-known TV gardening expert, Fred Streeter, was taken on to appear in TV and magazine advertisements. The fertiliser launch was at the Chelsea Flower Show at the Royal Hospital Grounds in the 1950s. The strapline was, 'Get to the Root of Things'.

The product sold very well and was a winner. Graham Farish was so pleased that he gave my father an upmarket TV. The set duly arrived, but my father decided he would sell it. He said it was not a good idea for young children's minds to be filled with such rubbish.

My next edition of Practical Television had an article on how to build you own TV. I decided to have a go. It was based on a radar set from a Lancaster Bomber. I found a shop in Praed Street selling government surplus from WW2 and I bought a radar set costing £2.

It was only later that I discovered how many sections were involved in obtaining a television picture. I copied out the wiring diagrams, marking in red when each piece of wiring had been completed.

The set contained 36 valves. I had to construct a separate set to pick up TV radio signals. I made it my bedroom and it took about six months to complete. The cathode ray tube (CRT) provided a six-inch green and white picture. I bought a later version of the CRT which was blue/grey and slightly bigger in size. I also bought a magnifier, which increased the size of the picture to about nine inches. You had to watch the picture full on, or it became very distorted. My set generated so much heat that I had to turn it off long before I went to bed.

Needless to say, my father did not carry out this threat to sell the TV he was given. When ITV started in 1956, he was quick to have the set converted to receive the second channel. My father was the principal user of the TV for the rest of his life.

With the change from 405 lines to 625 lines, my set became obsolete. There was no point in keeping it, I had achieved what I set out to do, so the waste disposal people took it away. It is now probably in a hole in the ground somewhere.

My father's set lasted a long time and was eventually replaced by a larger one. Being a compulsive gambler he used to watch it whenever a major horse race was on. The telephone was placed on top of the TV so he could watch the horses in the pre-race parade and then call his bookmaker. He always said that if a horse was sweating or decided to relieve itself, you should not back it. Despite these pearls of wisdom, he continued to lose money.

7.

Africa

In early 1962, having worked in the City of London, I was keen to travel and see something of the world. Africa, I thought, would be interesting. My place of work was within walking distance of Rhodesia House in the Strand. I went in during my lunch break and said I was keen on emigrating to what was then the Federation of Rhodesia and Nyasaland.

A receptionist gave me some information and suggested I come back soon for an interview. I went back two days later and was interviewed by two men, one British and the other Rhodesian. They asked me to formally apply by giving me forms to complete. I did this and a few days later was accepted. I was given a ticket for a flight from London Heathrow to Salisbury, the capital of the Federation.

I had not expected the reaction I received from my family. My mother was in tears, my father took to the gin bottle and my elder brother tried to dissuade me. He said a friend of his had just returned from working in South Africa and I would be murdered in my bed. It was a place to avoid. I pointed out that I was not going to South Africa but to the Federation of Rhodesia and Nyasaland.

When the day came for me to leave, I took a taxi to the BOAC air terminal in Victoria, accompanied by my parents. We took to drinking gin until it was time for me to go. I travelled from Victoria to Heathrow in a BOAC bus. I was allowed to take 60kg of luggage with me.

The flight in a BOAC 707 was uneventful, but an experience for me as I had not flown in a long-range plane before. When I arrived at Salisbury Airport there was an announcement over the tannoy for me to report to the Interline desk. My heart sank and I wondered what could have happened. I need not have worried. I was met by two people from the Ministry of Home Trade. They took me to the Windsor Hotel in the centre, where I had booked a room for a few days, and gave me a welcome lunch. The hotel was in the old colonial style, with large balconies and was very comfortable.

I was asked if I had obtained a job before leaving, which I had not done. They suggested that I come to their office at about 5pm, where they would start the process of finding me one. I was told I could use their office for making telephone calls and any secretarial services I might require.

After a good night's sleep and an excellent breakfast, I went back to their office. They suggested four well-known firms, along with the names of people I should contact. I phoned them and arranged to be interviewed. Although they were all pleased to see me, none had anything to offer.

I lowered my sights and went for more menial jobs. I got a job immediately with British American Tobacco (BAT) as a costing clerk. I would be working in an open-plan office of 16 people. I could not afford a car, but fortunately there was a company bus that ran from the city centre to the factory. Although I could not afford to stay long in the Windsor Hotel, I used to go there in the evening for cocktails and to listen to Edwin and Rachelle, a couple who sang songs of their own composing about local events.

In order to understand some of their lyrics, you would need to know something of the local goings-on. Petrol filling stations had started selling French Letters (condoms) mainly to Africans, who called them 'one night's pleasure'. At that time, Salisbury Cathedral of Mary and All Saints was officiated by the very Rev. Gonville ffrench-Beytagh. He was high church, very unpopular, and managed to empty the church rather quickly. He was waging a campaign to stop sales of condoms. Hence Edwin and Rachelle wrote a song that went as follows: 'If you think that copulation will increase the population, would it not be Beytagh if you used a ffrench letter?'

The Dean was removed by the Church from presiding over the cathedral. He had welcomed in blacks to worship, which led to his white parishioners going to another church. After being made Dean of Saint Mary's in Johannesburg, he was arrested by the Bureau of State Security (BOSS) in 1970 for once again allowing blacks in to his church. He was tried in August of that year, but released in November and left the country.

After working for BAT for six months, I thought I would look for a better job. I took a day off and visited four well-known firms on the industrial estate. After a tiring and unsuccessful day, I tried to visit the last firm on my list. The firm was the Metal Box Company of Central Africa Limited (MB). I gave my CV to the African on reception and he gave it to the Managing Director's secretary.

I took a taxi back to my new flat in the suburbs, which fortunately had a telephone. I hadn't been home long when the phone rang. I wondered who it could be as I hardly knew anyone in the city. It was the MD's secretary whom I had just met. She said the he liked my CV and wanted to meet me that afternoon. I explained that I did not have a car so she sent her boss's car to collect me. A short time later a large Hillman Imperial car arrived, driven by Ruben the chauffeur.

The MD was a very pleasant Anglo-Swiss man who had spent much of his working life in India. He had been looking for someone to join the company to sort out the problems they had with product quality. My CV seemed to fit the bill. He then talked as if I had already joined the company.

'Tell me, at school did you play soccer or rugby?' he asked.

'Rugby Sir,' I replied.'

'That's all right then,' he said. 'If you had said soccer I would not offer you a job.'

He then said he wanted me to fly to Bulawayo the following day to see MB's other factory. 'It is being run by somebody who thinks he knows it all. I will arrange for a ticket for you to collect at the airport.'

I was met at Bulawayo Airport by the manager of the factory, who previously had worked for the Colonial Office. He was clearly very competent and had overseen the building of the factory from the start. It produced open-top food cans on two lines, each producing five cans per second. He showed me around the factory, which was very impressive and had a good atmosphere. I was then given lunch, taken to the Matopos Hills to see the grave of British mining magnate and politician Cecil John Rhodes and then returned to the airport.

I had to give BAT four weeks' notice and started with MB on 1 April 1963. I spent my first few weeks working in the Salisbury factory. It made general line containers, mainly for paints, polishes and powered milk. The factory printed sheets of tinplate for both of MB's factories. My first job was to examine the quality of products, particularly concerning poor printing. I discovered that the Salisbury factory had management problems and a bad atmosphere.

For my next few weeks I was then sent to Bulawayo. The manager of the Bulawayo factory had returned to the UK with his family for a holiday. I went round to his house to see if everything was secure and, to my surprise, the house was completely empty – all the furniture had gone. I reported this to the MD in Salisbury. It turned out that the manager had been offered a good job in London with an American firm of management consultants, which he had accepted and never returned to Bulawayo.

This turned out to my advantage as I was put in charge of the factory as acting manager until a replacement could be found in the UK. A replacement arrived but he was not a success. The home company always sent those they could spare to their subsidiaries abroad, so you never got the best.

My training at MB consisted of spending time in their factories in South Africa, at Durban and Vanderbijl Park near Johannesburg. My stay at Vanderbijl Park factory was extremely unpleasant. All the staff were Afrikaners who resented my presence and refused to talk to me. At lunch they only spoke in Afrikaans. I wondered if they were still fighting the Boer War.

I was put up in the only local hotel and when I signed in, the manager was very unhelpful. He gave me a key to the room. I let myself in and found a man asleep in it. I went down to see the manager again and said the room was already taken. He said, 'You cannot expect the Ritz here, you will have to share.' I spent a very disturbed night in the same room as a man who snored his head off. I put up with this for two weeks, after which I was delighted to leave both the factory and the hotel.

I was then sent for further training in MB factories in Acton London, Worcester, Manchester, plus Palmers Green in London. These visits were set up by the MB Head office in Baker Street, London. I was amazed by what I experienced in some of the factories. The Palmers Green factory produced general line cans for paints, biscuits and polishes and was strongly unionised. I was shown around by a junior manager. In the printing shop, I was looking at some recent sheets of printed tinplate to see how they compared with ours. There was little difference, except that they did seem to waste tinplate in offcuts. One of the printers saw me and called the shop steward. I was told that it was not allowed for non-union employees to even look at their work. I was asked to leave.

The Manchester factory produced composite containers. These consisted of cardboard bodies spun on a mandrel, with tinplate tops and bottoms. It was possible to produce liquid-tight containers by including an impermeable liner beneath the cardboard body. I assisted in testing prototypes for such containers.

The Acton factory produced open-top food cans on a variety of lines, with speeds of five cans per second to 15 cans per second, depending on the age of the line. The plant also housed the research department, which had a staff of about 10 people. When I visited, I was appalled that no one was doing any work. Three were reading newspapers, two were permanently on the telephone and others were having a smoke or talking with mates. Another was frequently on the line to his bookmaker.

There was just one woman who appeared to be doing some work. She was putting what I took to be a trial dish in an oven to see if it was suitable for canning. I asked her about it. She said she was having a dinner party that evening and her oven at home was not big enough. She was therefore cooking her dinner at work using ingredients she had taken from the stores.

Back in the Salisbury factory, I had three Africans working for me in quality control. I decided to take them to a multi-racial hotel, The Park Lane, in the city, for my first Christmas in the country. Although such establishments were open to all races, many Africans did not like using such places because of the verbal abuse some received from white customers.

When we got to the hotel, the three did not want to enter because they thought they would not be allowed in. Fortunately a group of Europeans and Africans arrived and went straight in. So we went in as well. After the first drink they relaxed and all was well. They were most grateful.

I realised that I would need to get a driving licence. I had my UK one, which was accepted as sufficient for them to issue a Rhodesian licence. It had my photo in it, with a place for a signature or right thumb print. It was usable in most countries in the world, cost 10 shillings (50 pence) and was for life. I still have it as a souvenir.

8.

The Metal Box Company Ltd

The company dates from 1921, when about 30 mainly family-owned makers of tins were under threat from a company called American Can. This US company decided to open a factory in Ealing, West London, to make food cans which, up until this point, had to be imported. The UK family firms made general line tins used mainly for paints, floor polish, boot polish and a range of tins for other products. They required much hand work in their construction.

American Can intended to use machines in their London venture that could produce food cans at a fast speed. These machines had been designed by another American firm called Troyer-Fox, which was bought by US firm Continental Can just before World War Two.

One of the UK firms, Barlow Brothers, had a dynamic chief executive who was able to convince his competitors that they should merge in order to be in a position to fight off American Can. After much debate this was agreed and Metal Box came into existence.

The new UK company did a deal with Continental Can to provide them with equipment, training and expertise. The UK newcomers were very successful and within a year were able to buy out American Can's Ealing plant and to obtain an agreement that they would not try to enter the UK market again for a period of 40 years.

Married to actress Margaret Rawlings, Robert Barlow (1891-1976) was the architect of Metal Box's phenomenal success. He approached bottle top manufacturers Crown Cork in Southall and agreed that Metal Box would not make Crown Corks for 40 years. In return, they would not produce cans for 40 years. Continental Can agreed with Metal Box that they would keep out of operating in Britain and countries in the British Empire and Commonwealth, while Metal Box agreed that they would not operate in the Americas.

Metal Box set up their headquarters in Baker Street London. Subsidiaries were also set up in South Africa, Kenya, Tanganyika, Malaya, India, and in what is now Bangladesh. The last subsidiary was my old company, Metal Box Company of Central Africa. They also took minor stakes in most of the Western European can makers. They tried to operate in Italy but the firm, called Superbox, was not a success. They found it necessary to operate profitably only if they kept the tax man on side by means of brown envelopes. Superbox did not last long.

UK shareholders did very well out of MB's shares. The company was a spectacular success and the share price made it into a Blue Chip. Apart from success on the stock market, shareholders would receive a hamper of tins and canned goods from the company at Christmas time. This had to be dropped after a while as it was becoming abused by would-be shareholders who would buy five shares solely to receive a hamper.

My time with the company in Central Africa was enjoyable. They were a nice firm to work for and they really looked after their staff. In 1970 the headquarters of the group was moved to a brand new building in Reading named Queen's House. It occupied a huge site close to Reading railway station and had been built in such a way that it could have more storeys added to it. However, competition had forced it to shrink in size and eventually it was demolished, to be replaced by two tall buildings.

Having worked for Metal Box in Central Africa before, during and after UDI, (the taking of independence by a unilateral declaration), the group assured me they would look after me when the time came for me to return to UK. They would, I was assured, find me a good position in the home company.

But when the time came, the home company said they knew nothing about me and I would have to start at the bottom. The only possible job they could offer was working with quality control in Neath South Wales – on the night shift. I turned it down immediately.

Some time later, things started to go wrong for MBC, beginning with the retirement of Robert Barlow as chief executive. Barlow was an autocrat who had recruited a small group of yes-men

around him. After Barlow's departure, they took over as chief executive one by one. By this time they were close to retirement and did not want to make any decisions that could jeopardise their last few years.

But the can-making industry was changing rapidly. The three-piece can was being replaced by a one-piece body with a loose top and easy-opening cans were now being demanded by many customers. Apart from baked beans and dog food, demand for food cans was falling fast as the popularity of frozen food was growing. To make matters worse, the 40-year exclusion negotiated with American Can and Crown Cork came to an end and they could now make cans in the UK.

The can market was also changing. The demand was now for cans for beer, mixers and soft drinks which requires totally different technology to cans for foodstuffs.

The result of all these changes meant that customers could now shop around between suppliers and none of the can makers were making a profit. Amalgamations took place and Metal Box was taken over by Carnaud of France to become Carnaud Metalbox. This was not a success and the company was acquired by Crown Cork and Seal. What was left of the old company tried to diversify and became Ideal Stelrad, merging with Ideal boilers and radiators. In my opinion, they should have been looking instead at other aspects of packaging, such as glass, plastics, paper and card. To me, this seemed like a sad end to a once famous and successful company.

9.

Bulawayo

Towards the end of my time as manager of the Metal Box plant in Bulawayo, I thought I would do something to try to improve the education of some of the brightest indigenous Matabele. I set up a school in the factory's canteen. The education they received at state schools took them up to a level where they could understand English and do simple arithmetic. There was, however, a keen ambition to learn more. I asked the man responsible for black recruitment to let people know that a school was being set up. To my amazement, we received so many applicants that we had to limit it and entry was decided by interview with the African schoolmaster I had recruited. He would teach English and Arithmetic, while I would do General Knowledge on subjects of their choosing. If I could not do it, I would find a someone who could.

There was a great wish to know something about our planet. I drew a circle on the blackboard to represent the earth. I was asked why I had drawn a circle as the earth was flat. They all agreed that the earth was flat and said that you just had to look out of the window to know that. I said the best way to demonstrate this was to consider a ship at sea. As a ship came over the horizon, you could see the curvature of the earth. However, Rhodesia was a land-locked state, so none of them had seen the sea. They could not believe that anyone could consider the earth to be round.

Their next question was, 'Where do you mine plastics'? Rhodesia was a mining country so they knew where copper and other minerals were mined. They could not believe that a raw material could be manmade.

The next incredulous discussion revolved around a moon shoot, where a man had been shot into the stratosphere. I tried to describe about re-entry but got nowhere. One asked, if he had gone up in a rocket he would have gone to Heaven, so why did God let him out?

MD's Last visit

At this point the schoolmaster decided to make a change and join another school. This was a great relief to me and made me realise that education consists of two parts; what you learn from your parents and what you learn at school. I was attempting to give them part two, but the parents probably knew even less than their children.

My managing director was at the point of retiring, and he made his last visit to the Bulawayo branch of the company to say goodbye. I arranged for a group photograph to be taken and we also gave him a leaving present. He told us that he had decided to live in Tasmania, Australia.

Unrest in the East

At that time there was some unrest in the Eastern part of the country where a few Europeans had been murdered. People between the ages of 18 and 65 were told to register for military service in case this became necessary. I received a card saying that I was a private in the 30th battalion of the Royal Rhodesian Regiment.

About 35 of us had to parade at the Exchange Bar one Friday evening each month. We were issued with Lee-Enfield rifles. However, I was the only person who had handled one and knew how to use it. I assumed the role of sergeant and taught them how to use this weapon and also the basics of drill.

The Exchange Bar was probably the oldest building in Bulawayo and was originally the Stock Exchange and where gold could be bought and sold. It was now a bar run by Cyril. After about 30 minutes Cyril announced that the bar was open. At that moment I lost my whole platoon: having a drink was more important than playing solders.

Central African Trade Fair

Every other year, the Central African Trade Fair was held in Bulawayo. Run by Zoe Shearer, a very dynamic organiser, it was always well attended and provided a shop window for Rhodesian goods.

I booked a stand for my company, the Metal Box Company of Central Africa, to display our wares. To look after it, I recruited a rather glamorous barmaid called Libbie whom I had met at a bar in the city centre. By way of preparation, I had shown her round the factory, explaining exactly what we did, gave her pamphlets on food canning and said we would buy her a new dress to wear.

The fair opened at 8am, so I made sure I was there. The first person I met was the Prime Minister, Ian Smith. There was no sign of Libbie. I telephoned her and was told she had overslept. By lunchtime she had not arrived. I telephoned her again and was told she did not have any shoes to wear. The ones she had did not match the dress. Could we let her have new shoes?

She arrived just as the fair was closing. We had a range of our cans as dummies, they were supposed to be empty and with both ends on. I was showing a can to a prospective customer and realised it was full, as were all the other cans on display.

Libbie was a single mother with little money to spare. She had been round the stands of firms who used our cans and swapped their filled cans with our dummies so she could eventually take the full cans home. It was a relief when the fair closed. When the show was over, Libbie telephoned me saying she had no money. I said I could not help directly but I knew a couple who were going on long leave to the UK and needed someone to look after their house. She met them and seemed to get on well. They did not mind her bringing the child or the dog. When they returned, the house was in a mess and the dog had died.

Anyone for Tennis?

Every year the staff at Kamativi Tin Mine invited a team from Bulawayo to visit, during which we would play cricket, tennis and be shown around the mine. We would also be well fed and agreeably drunk for the two days we were there. The mine was situated to the North-West of Bulawayo. I was interested to see it as it produced cassiterite, the principal ore of tin. We made our tins and cans from tinplate, which consists of steel with a thin coating of tin.

After seeing the mine and the extracting process we played tennis without disgracing ourselves. We did not fare so well in the afternoon when, after an excellent lunch, we had to play their side at cricket. We were well beaten due to lack of practice and too much to drink. We enjoyed an excellent two days there and I think our hosts enjoyed seeing some new faces.

My game of tennis improved during my time in Bulawayo. There was a boys preparatory school outside the city and I had the good luck to meet the headmaster who was a keen tennis player. A group of friends met on Wednesday afternoons to play on one of the school's courts. I was invited to join them. After a while I started to improve and could hold my own in games of doubles.

Someone said I should meet a Colonel Cousins who had been an officer in the Gurkhas and now coached tennis. He had played most of his life and met his wife while playing at Wimbledon. He was now in his sixties and I thought he was too old to be a tennis coach. His style was most extraordinary. He had a folding stool which he placed on the service line. Next to him he had an adjustable machine that fired balls at you. There were two Africans on the court to collect the balls. If the boy supposed to be filling up the ball hopper wasn't concentrating, the colonel would shout, 'Willard!', followed by a well-aimed ball. Despite his unusual way of coaching he help me a lot and I was able to master the overhead smash. He then entered me for a competition, which is something I would never have dreamed of doing. The matches were for mixed doubles. What amazed me was that he had ball boys on the court. I had never seen that outside Wimbledon. At the end of the match the ball boys would be paid a tickey (a threepenny coin).

The Colonel spent his time arguing with his wife. I heard later that they had divorced. She returned to England and he settled in Durban in South Africa. I heard later he had remarried a girl who was 30 years his junior.

During my time in South Africa I also played tennis at the Inanda Polo Club in Johannesburg, thanks to my membership of the Hurlingham Club in London. Back in Bulawayo I knew many people who had their own courts and, being single, it was not difficult to find a game at weekends. Although I did play again when back in the UK, I found it difficult once the effects of polio, which I contracted at the age of 12, started to affect me. I managed to keep playing until I reached the age of 60.

Flying Fruit and Swimming Snakes

Quite early in my time in Rhodesia I was invited to spend a weekend on a tobacco farm. My contact was the sister of a woman my mother knew in UK. Her son had emigrated to Rhodesia in the 1950s and bought a plot of land with a loan from the Land Bank. The light soil was suitable for growing tobacco but there was much work to be done in order to turn the land into a farm. First he had to clear the bundu (wild countryside) of trees and scrub in order to create suitable growing conditions.

He also had to dam a stream to impound water, build housing for the workers and set up a school for their children. He had plans to eventually build a house for himself, wife and family. In the meantime, they were living in a large mud hut with a thatched roof the workers had built for them. It was extremely primitive, with no electric lighting and no piped water. The internal walls were about 6 feet tall which meant that when I (at 6ft 3in) stood in the guest room I could see everything going on in all the other rooms.

I discovered I had a distant cousin and her family living outside Salisbury. They lived at the top of a kopje (hill) and had built a very pleasant house with a terraced garden below it. The only problem was that you had to negotiate a very steep, narrow, ungraded track to get there. In the rainy season it was impassable. There were other houses on this track and you just hoped that no one was coming in the opposite direction, otherwise one of you would have to back up.

Me in the Bundu

I had never met my cousin Valerie before, but I got to know her and her husband and three children very well. On one occasion she was having a lunch party and was in a panic. She could not find the key to the drinks cabinet. African staff are very keen on alcohol and so people had to keep their drink under lock and key. The only thing left was to ask Moses the cook if he knew where the key was. 'No madam,' he replied. 'But why do you not do as we do and take the back off the cabinet?' Moses went back to the kitchen and returned with a screwdriver.

On another occasion when I was staying with them, Valerie wanted to pick some paw paw fruit from trees she had planted sometime before. She went outside and was met with a fusillade of over-ripe paw paws, stones and mealie (sweetcorn) cobs, thrown by baboons who were presumably taking exception to someone else trying to take their snacks. She had to beat a hasty retreat and decided to get her paw paws and mealies from a farm stall in future.

Their nearest neighbour liked to have swim in his pool after coming in from a hard day's work. There was a tree overhanging one corner of the pool. After a short while he heard a splash and a green mamba fell out of the tree and into the water, making straight for him. He reckoned he broke the world record as he swam to the side and got out. Fortunately the snake had some difficulty in getting out of the pool and did not follow.

When I was living in Johannesburg I shared a flat with Bill, another management consultant. All the ex-pat consultants were entitled to have a small Fiat 124 car provided by our firm. Bill wanted something bigger so bought a Volvo. The time came for its first service. A car from the garage arrived with two drivers. The second driver was to drive Bill's car back to the garage.

The first driver drove off. To his horror, Bill saw his car doing a number of kangaroo leaps down the drive. He rushed out and asked the second driver what the problem was. 'I don't think you know how to drive,' said Bill.

The answer came back, 'No master, but I am learning.'

'Not in my car you're not,' replied Bill. A strong complaint was made to the garage.

10.

Mozambique

When I was living in Rhodesia, a long weekend in Mozambique made a very pleasant change of scenery. The first time I went there it was a Portuguese colony, with the capital being Lorenzo Marques (LM), now renamed Maputu.

To give a bit of history: when Salazar was president of Portugal and its territories, he tried to maintain a 10 per cent ratio of Europeans to Africans. They also had to cope with a civil war with the Frelimo guerillas who, supported by the Russians, were trying to set up a Marxist state. Many young Portuguese were conscripted into the army and were sent from mainland Portugal to fight this guerilla threat. At its peak, some 30,000 troops were involved in fighting Frelimo.

There was growing resentment back home that taxes had been raised to finance the war. On the death of Salazar, the new president Caetano gave independence to Mozambique on the East coast and Angola on the West coast of Africa. A period of turmoil ensued in mainland Portugal, during which Caetano was overthrown and the country degenerated into civil war. Fortunately, this did not last for very long.

It was an easy drive from Salisbury (Harare) to Umtali (Mutari) and then over the border into Mozambique. We broke the journey there and had coffee to drink. At the next table was a man hiding behind a newspaper. When I stood up I recognised him as someone I knew in Bulawayo. He was hiding from his creditors and he appeared regularly in Dun's Gazette.

Porto Bridge

In Mozambique, we had the choice of going to either Beira, a busy sea port, or to LM the capital city. Unlike Portugal and its other African colonies, they drive on the left in order to be the same as other countries in Southern Africa.

The first time I visited the country, I had been asked to take Jim, a member of Head Office in London, who was visiting the Rhodesian company to do a management audit. This was more of a spot check rather than a financial audit.

Jim was an accountant by training and an ex-management consultant. He managed to annoy every senior member of the company by his incessant questioning. This interested me a lot, as I was planning a move into management consultancy when the time came for me to move back to the UK. Our Mozambique trip was therefore very useful for me to learn from him.

I had booked two rooms for us at the Polana Hotel in LM, which turned out to be an excellent hotel with good cuisine. LM was known for its shellfish. I did not know at the time this was due to the drainage system, which contaminated the whole bay. At dinner that evening I ordered some prawns. The waiter asked me how many I wanted. I said about six. Without a word he disappeared and came back with one prawn on a dinner plate. It was about the size of a lobster but without its claws. The next day we went to a bistro for lunch and I ordered a crab. It was the biggest crab I had ever seen. Shellfish, being scavengers, were thriving on pollution in the bay.

The Author at Lorenzo Marques

We then drove to Gorongosa National Park game reserve. It was the best one I had ever been to, largely because the Portuguese were not overly worried about safety. In most game reserves you have to stay in your car, but in this one you could get out of your vehicle and walk around. I was keen to see a lion, and the guide said he knew where to find some. I had previously seen all the other Big Five in other game reserves, but no lions. He found two lions but they were asleep, having just fed on their prey. I said that a lion asleep was no good to me. I wanted to photograph one awake. Our guide got out of the car and twisted one of the lion's ears. It woke up with a roar so I got my photo.

Accommodation in the reserve was in thatched rondavels. These are based on African huts, but with modern amenities such as ensuite facilities and air conditioning.

After the game reserve we travelled north to Senna Sugar Estate. A girl I knew from Bulawayo had recently married the manager of the estate and they gave us a good welcome.

Years later, when I was a management consultant, I did an assignment in a sugar beet factory in the UK. I found it very interesting to see how sugar is produced from cane, as opposed to beet. In fact, it is quite different.

With sugar cane, the cut sugar cane is transported to a large, flat concrete floor and then emptied and spread evenly. Cane is then removed for processing from around the edges of the spread cane until there is only a little left in the centre. This not only contains the cane, but also any undesirables such as snakes, cane toads, weeds and other contaminants.

For many years sugar was produced from sugar cane in the West Indies. However, because of blockades, a way had to be found to produce sugar in the UK. Sugar beet was found to be suitable, with a similar sugar content to cane. Initially it provided about half the UK's sugar requirements. Processing sugar beet is first done by washing the beet in flumes, then slicing and extraction of the raw sugar. The washed soil is dried and bagged and sold back to farmers and horticulturists.

On our way home from the sugar estate we stopped to visit a customer in Cashel. I knew the manager well and he seemed very pleased to see us. They produced canned fruit and vegetables and were one of our best customers. He told the head office visitor that we gave them excellent service. We also stopped at a farm producing mushrooms. The farmer there said he had no complaints except that I was a difficult person to deal with.

I realised from the questions I had been asked that there was more to our trip than I had originally expected. The visiting consultant wanted to see whether I was suitable management material to be considered for future promotion. I think I passed.

My brother John visited me twice in Rhodesia and each time we visited the Eastern Districts. You had to travel through them on the way to Mozambique. On one of these visits we visited some of the places near the border. These included Troutbeck, Leopard Rock and Birchenough.

I spent my first Christmas in Rhodesia in 1962 with friends of my parents who lived in a place called Penhalonga. My host was responsible for reporting the area's weather conditions to the government. No one could understand why rainfall in the area was significantly higher than in neighbouring areas, so they sent a weather specialist to investigate.

The family had a very nice retriever dog. It was then discovered that the dog relieved himself by using the rain gauge, which resulted in abnormal rain figures for the immediate area.

In the Eastern Districts there are numerous small rivers crossed by low-level bridges. These were constructed between the wars as a rapid way to open up the country. The bridges are submerged in the rainy season but in summer, when there is very little water in the river, they are easy to cross.

However, when the bridges are covered, many people have found that a car can be pushed off a bridge by the pressure of the water. My first car in Rhodesia was a 1947 VW Beetle, which I bought with 80,000 miles on the clock. They are primitive in design and my car did not have a petrol gauge. The lever for the jack could be used as a dipstick to see how much petrol was left and the electrics were supplied by a six-volt battery. It did, however, have a reserve tank of one gallon. When you ran out of fuel, a lever near your left foot would bring the reserve tank into action.

Despite my Beetle's lack of sophistication, it proved most useful when visiting the Eastern Districts because of its ability to float. If driving over a bridge when it was underwater, you had to open both doors to allow the water to flow in. This weighed it down so that it stayed on the bridge. Even better, the mats were rubber so there were no carpets to spoil.

The Beatle

11.

Madeira

The Author

The island of Madeira lies about 300 miles from the African coast and 550 miles from Europe. It is considered to be part of mainland Portugal and is self-governing. The island is dominated by an extinct volcano in the central part of the island. Most of the development is along the southern coastal part facing the sea, with a very active port. Funchal is the capital, with the port at its centre. Its permanent population is around a quarter of a million, which swells in peak holiday time to over a million.

Madeira is fortunate in having a sub-tropical climate. I have been there in August, November, January and February and have always been able to sunbathe and swim. The first time I visited the island was on my way from Cape Town in South Africa on a Saga cruise. Funchal was the first stop on the voyage home to Southampton. Our visit coincided with the New Year fireworks display, which were the best I had ever seen.

My Brother, David

The next time I visited Madeira was in November 1989. I had just sold my scientific consultancy to one of the privatised water companies. I had not had a decent holiday for some time and had money in my pocket. I went with an old friend and we stayed in Reid's Hotel. I had heard about the hotel but had not appreciated how luxurious it was and how many famous people had stayed there.

My elder brother David had not been well for some time and was confined to a wheelchair. I decided to treat him and his wife to an eight-day holiday at the hotel. The food and service were superb. I particularly remember our first breakfast. I was having my cereal when I dropped the spoon on the floor. I went to pick it up, but a waiter's hand got there first. When I sat up, another waiter's hand was already placing a clean spoon on the table.

Monte

Toboggan Run

My sister-in-law and I decided to do the toboggan run from the top of Monte, where a large church was a popular tourist place to visit, down to sea level. My brother was limited in what he could do, which meant he could not take the cable car up or down. Toboggans are made of a wicker seat with hardwood runners for two people. To make the run, two men looking like Venetian gondoliers stand on the back to control the toboggan. It is downhill all the way along the main road, luckily missing parked cars and pedestrians, and takes about 30 minutes at a speed of about 30mph. I did the run again more recently in 2020 with a friend.

Before the cable car was installed, there was a steam-driven train to take people up to Monte, with stops on the way. Unfortunately, on one journey the locomotive exploded, killing many people. The remains of the line can still be seen near the top. It was replaced by the cable car.

Dinner in the evening was available at many restaurants in our hotel. In the main dining room, the dress code was black tie. More than once a member of staff would take over the role of pushing my brother in his wheelchair to relieve my sister-in-law of the task.

We hired a car and driver and visited much of the island. This included visits to the north, which is sparsely populated and has a different climate to the rest of the island.

Michael   *Me*

My last journey to Madeira was in November 2020, once again staying at Reid's. To me the idea of staying there was to experience a way of life which, in most places, no longer existed. It is not the way I would want to live, but it was a treat to experience the way people used to live, including many famous names. Winston Churchill used to paint there and George Bernard Shaw was famously taught to dance the tango in the hotel. It was also popular with deposed royalty and heads of state.

But on my last visit there, the hotel had recently changed hands and sadly was no longer the hotel I used to know. The famous dining room was only open two evenings per week and, instead of the smart dress code, some diners were wearing jeans and T-shirts. I thought that their next step would be to display a notice saying, 'coach parties welcome'. Some of the old retainers were understandably very upset in the way the hotel had been allowed to change. The service, which used to be excellent, was now appalling.

On most of my visits to Madeira, I used to dine one night in a restaurant in the old town, which had been highly praised in Winner's Dinners column in the Sunday Times. Michael Winner was a film producer who loved his food. The restaurant was in the Old Town of Funchal and was called Cosemios Restaurant, located at 169 Rue do Santa Maria. Even after Winner had died, the restaurant displayed a framed copy of the newspaper's article.

Reid's was known for its magnificent gardens. While some of the land had been sold off for building flats, I was pleased to see that much of it remains and were well maintained as before.

There are frequent flights from UK to Funchal operated by British Airways, Easyjet and TAP Portugal's own airline. The airport was one of the most dangerous in the world due to its very short runway. Aircraft coming into land had to get the approach just right or they would overshoot. The runway has been lengthened at both ends in recent years, with the extensions consisting of concrete piers over the sea to carry the extensions. Even so, the runway is still considered to be too short. To the north of the runway there is a large mountain. Planes cannot land in windy weather as there is always a risk of being blown into it.

Runway risks aside, I will go there again as it is one of my favourite holiday destinations. It is certainly one of the friendliest places I know. I would not stay at Reid's again, but I would go there for a drink to see if it had improved.

12.

Wellington College

I left Forres, my preparatory school in Swanage, at the end of the Lent term 1949 and joined Wellington at the start of the summer term. I must say I had mixed feelings about leaving my old school. I felt as if I had outgrown it, but at the same time I was apprehensive about facing new pupils and new routines.

On my first day my parents drove me down to Crowthorne for tea with the House Master. There were five boys there, each with their parents. One by one, the House Master asked us what our feelings were and what we hoped to get out of this new experience. I said I wanted to receive a good education, become less shy and loose my stammer.

I studied the other parents carefully. One was an old Etonian who did not speak kindly of his old school. I had the feeling that he had a chip on his shoulder. I found out later that he had shipped his two sons off to the USA for the war, which grated on me as I had had to spend most of the war in London, where I was bombed out twice. My mother was intrigued that this Etonian wore a jacket with brass buttons. She thought he looked like a chauffeur.

One boy ~~was ex-navy and~~ the son of the King's press secretary, while another one said his ambition was to inherit his family's stately home in Cumberland and keep it in the family. The parents of the next new boy were rather flash and the first thing I thought of was new money. I was wrong. His father had also been to Wellington and had been in the army. At that point, matron joined us for tea. I immediately thought of Hattie Jacques. I held back the tears when my parents left.

Matron then showed us to our rooms, which were small and separated by wooden partitions that did not go all the way up to the ceiling. It was a beatable offence to 'tish pop' – to look over the partitions to your neighbour.

Each new boy had a coach to show him the ropes. At the end of two weeks you had a fag's examination to see if you had learnt about the school, including all nicknames for the teachers. If you did not pass, your coach was beaten.

It was assumed that you would now be ready to be a fag. A better title would be slave. New boys were lined up so each prefect could choose who he wanted as his servant. It was therefore prefects of 17 or 18, young men soon to be fighting for their King and country, who were choosing 13-year-old boys reaching puberty to be their servant. They were not chosen on their bed-making ability. Those not chosen by a prefect became general fags, who would do all the dirty jobs. I was a general fag.

One of my intake, the one whom I thought was very flash, turned out to be a bully. Food was still being rationed and parents used to help out by sending eggs, pots of home-made marmalade and other edibles. My mother always used to make me a cake.

The bully would sit down and say he was hungry. Then he would help himself to what he wanted, which meant some of us had to go without. We got so fed up we started to think of ways to get our own back. We saw our chance when the bully let it slip that his parents would be visiting on the following Saturday.

Myself and another from my intake decided we would trash his room. We did not break anything, but emptied the contents of his chest of drawers onto the floor, upended the bed, took down pictures and generally left the room in a shambles.

We then saw the parents and son coming down the passage. We hid in anticipation. There was a shriek from the mother, mock laughter from the father and tears from the son. I thought it would be prudent to go out for the rest of the afternoon.

At evening prayers the House Master said he was appalled when he heard what had happened and would those responsible report to his study immediately after prayers. The two of us duly went to his study and, to our amazement, were accompanied by six others.

The House Master asked who was responsible. The two of us owned up, along with two others, who said they were also involved. The other four said if they had known about it they would have done the same. I expected to be beaten, but it became obvious that he could not beat all of us. So we were let off with a warning.

The effect on the bully was extraordinary. He changed his ways completely and became a different person, no longer selfish. Our rather rudimentary tactics had certainly worked.

I stayed a total of six years in the Federation of Rhodesia and Nyasaland. I was living in Salisbury, capital city of the Federation, when I heard that my old school, Wellington, was having one of its dinners. Held in the Salisbury Club, it was an annual affair for old boys only and it was a black-tie affair.

The timing of this was in early 1964. The Federation had just been disbanded, Northern Rhodesia and Nyasaland having been told that they would achieve independence in September. In the meantime, they were still Crown Colonies.

There was a tradition at the dinner that the youngest member present had to make a speech. I looked around and it was obviously me by about 25 years. The chairman asked me to tell them about college, as most of the members had not visited the old place for many years.

On my last visit to Wellington on Speech Day in 1963, the guest of honour was the War Minister, John Profumo and his wife Valerie Hobson. This was at the time when the Profumo scandal was starting to hit the headlines. I tried to make a joke about it by referring to him as the Minister of Whore.

This produced a howl of protest and I was told this was in very bad taste. Sitting opposite me was Brigadier Dunlop, the Rhodesian Minister of Transport, Brig. Skeene who had been the Rhodesian representative in London and Brig. Barstow who had lived in the country for many years and who clearly liked his drink. I could feel that I was not going down very well with this audience.

Brig. Dunlop said his job used to be easy, but now he had to deal with 'that black monkey' to the north of us in Zambia. I said that while I could understand his feeling, both he and the Zambian minister were subjects of the Crown until independence was achieved later in the year and he should not be referring to him that way.

'You young puppy!' he roared. 'How dare you speak to me like that?' There was general agreement all round.

I was then asked about my attitude to the blacks. I said I would like to see more done to advance the education of the indigenous population. 'As a successful country', I said, 'Rhodesia will need to train up brighter blacks as the supply of white immigrants has slowed right down.'

There was another howl of protest from almost everyone. One said, 'It's a shame Lord Graham isn't here, he would have put you right'. He was referring to one of Smith's cabinet ministers. Lord Graham was the title he used in Rhodesia, his real title was the Duke of Montrose.

I tried to explain further, but was told to go back to the UK. Someone said, 'That's a good idea, just go'. At that point I left. It was noticeable that I was not asked back to a reunion in later years.

The man sitting next to me had not said a word. Next day he telephoned me and said he wanted to apologise for not supporting me. He had agreed with every word I said. He then asked me to have lunch with him, which I accepted. He said that he had accepted a job offer with the World Bank and I wished him well.

Years later, when thinking about this dinner, I realised that I had been rather unfair to many of the diners, who were a lot older than me. They were all farmers who had come out from the UK between the wars and had created farms out of virgin bundu (bush), helped build roads, provided work for indigenous people and produced food for local consumption and export. Some had fought in World War Two. I had been in the country for about 18 months and knew little about it. I realised that I should get my facts right in future before speaking out.

School days

On my first morning at Wellington College, I went to the classroom for new boys in Upper 3A, the A stream being for the brighter boys. A cousin on my mother's side had also joined the school in the same term and went into the same class. My mother was always saying that he was bright and a lot brighter than me. At the end of the first term I came about six places higher than him in the class. That killed any further discussion.

The teachers, called ushers, were generally a mixture. The younger ones had served in World War Two and two of the older ones in the Great War. The younger ones could be aggressive, proud of what they had done in the war, or resentful for what the war had done to them.

Our usher for Upper 3A had had a successful army career and hated the Germans. He was particularly hard on me for having a German surname. I do not think anyone in the class really liked him. We had an usher who was going to teach us physics but it was obvious that he was suffering badly from shell shock. Some pupil had written on the blackboard, 'Maughan, Maughan would never have been born if his mother had known the rubber was torn.' It was very sad to see someone in such bad shape mentally. He had to be treated for his shell shock and it was some time before he returned to teaching, but not at Wellington.

Another usher, who taught us chemistry, clearly liked his drink. If a pupil was asked a question and got it wrong he would say, 'You stupid little gubbins'. One of the older ushers had a dog called Boxer, who attended all his master's lectures. Boxer was very old and could not control his bodily functions. He kept breaking wind and the air became suffocating. Not surprisingly, no one looked forward to chemistry classes.

Like many public schools, those who were good at sports were the favoured pupils. This put me somewhat at a disadvantage. Having had polio (infantile paralysis) two years earlier, I was limited in what I could do by way of sporting activities. I had to think of alternatives. Two things I really liked were art classes and learning to play the piano. I did not want to play classical music, but more popular tunes. My teacher was a great fan of Carroll Gibbons, an American who came to the UK in the1920s and had a very distinct way of playing, with a strong left hand. I was able to absorb what I had been taught during those lessons and enjoyed following my piano teacher's advice. Unfortunately, in old age I have lost the ability to play.

I had always been interested in natural history and I was even more keen to join the Natural History Society when I heard that members could keep a bicycle in their house. The Society had many rejected applicants who knew nothing about the subject but simply wanted to get a bicycle permit. Fortunately for me, I knew much about butterflies and so got my permit, along with a request to give a talk on the subject. Having a bike gave me freedom and many people wanted to borrow it. On occasions it was being used without my permission, so it had to be secured with a large padlock.

Talbot, my school house, was sited in grounds away from the main college block and was not popular with other houses who referred to it as 'the Plush Buggers' Suite'. We regarded their attitude as jealousy. Our house had its own kitchen, unlike the main houses in the central building, which had a central canteen serving all the colleges. We also had our own tennis court so we did not have to play on the courts used by everyone else.

The College was founded in 1863 as a memorial to The Duke of Wellington. It had been suggested that a statue to the Iron Duke be erected in every market town in the UK. But many market towns already had statues to old monarchs and local worthies. It was then suggested that a memorial should take the form of a school for the sons of officers who had fallen at Waterloo.

A plot of land was donated by a well wisher as a place to build the school. His intentions were not altogether altruistic. He knew the donated land would prove to be too small, so he offered to let them buy a neighbouring piece of land he owned at an exorbitant price.

The college was built and the intake widened to include children of army officers killed in any conflict. The college dormitories were named after Wellington's generals at Waterloo. Houses outside the main block were the exception. They were named Stanley, Talbot and Benson, after famous people of the time.

After World War Two, Attlee's labour government wanted to soak the rich and he despised fee-paying schools. Such schools were ordered to take a quota of boys from state schools and were paid for by the state. We had six pupils from London schools on what was called the Guinea Pig Scheme. The Master of Wellington delegated six pupils to help the new boys settle in to their new environment. After six weeks, four of the state schoolboys hated it so much that they went home. The two left were a success, although it must have been very difficult for them.

In terms of punishment, the school regime was pretty tough for all of us. At Wellington you could be beaten for the most minor offence. It was very easy to earn a thrashing if you said the wrong thing, as one boy discovered. He was building an electronic organ and one day an usher asked him, 'How's your organ?' The boy answered, 'Fine sir, how's yours?'

Fagging, whereby younger pupils were the servants of older boys, was another feature of Wellington life, as it was in every boarding school at the time. During my second term there, a new boy had just joined the house. He was aged 13 and was enjoying the new sensation of puberty. He was chosen to be a personal fag to an 18-year-old prefect who was still a virgin. The prefect was about to be called up for National Service to serve his King and Country. He had not been able to experience female company and, with testosterone levels being high, was feeling very frustrated with life.

He and his fag got on very well. The young lad liked having someone who was bright and intelligent, while the 18-year-old found the younger boy very attractive and was keen to teach him what he had discovered about life. A close relationship followed. Unfortunately, the news got out and the prefect was removed from being a prefect and then, once his parents had been informed, was removed from the school.

Most Wellingtonians went to Sandhurst and had an army career after that, but the expelled boy did not want to go into the army for fear of rejection,. About 10 years later, I saw that he had married a well-connected girl and was doing well in the City. Fortunately, attitudes have changed since then.

Wellington in Tianjin, China

The first international Wellington school was opened in the Chinese city of Tianjin in 2011. There are now five sister schools in China and one in Thailand. All are leading schools in their region, producing good examination results, with some of its students going on to win places at world-class universities.

Wellington in Bangkok, Thailand

13.

Adventures in Oz

One of my clients was a firm of American loss adjusters. My role was to supply a scientific input to the loss adjuster handling the case. You could receive a call at short notice and be asked to be anywhere in the world as quickly as possible to assist in handling the claim. The most common reason was the result of a fire, but it could be due to water damage, hail, or in one case, earthquake damage. I was to provide the scientific input when asked and not to talk to the insured directly, unless the loss adjuster requested it.

My first visit to Australia was to assist with a claim resulting from a freak storm that hit Sydney with hailstones the size of cricket balls. These had caused severe damage to cars, breaking windows and creating dents. During the storm, a warehouse had lost a large part of its asbestos roof, releasing asbestos fibres into the atmosphere. This was causing a hazard to employees and people living nearby. The firm produced drugs and other medicaments, some of which had to be stored in a temperature-controlled warehouse. Unfortunately, some of the stored items had been damaged when the warehouse lost its roof.

I realised that the job would be big, so I asked if one of my staff could assist. He arrived two days later, bringing a high-powered microscope suitable for detecting asbestos, its presence and the type.

Sydney Harbour Bridge

I was also assigned a former employee who knew the company backwards and I thought he could be a great help. However, whilst he knew the company and its products, he was one of the laziest people I have ever met. He arrived late, went early and took two hours for lunch. In the end I asked for him to be removed as he was stopping me and my assistant from working. We could make better progress without him.

I discovered that the damage to cars due to large hailstones had been faked by some. These cars tended to have damage to the roof and both sides. In reality, the hailstones were heavy due to their size and tended to travel straight down, therefore wouldn't do much damage to the sides. I caught one faker who had cut a cricket ball in half and then fixed it a piece of wood. He was using this to produce the dents. About 30 per cent of damage to cars was done by the owner and hence were not covered by insurance.

The damaged warehouse roof consisted of about 10 per cent white asbestos (chrysotile), which is typical for corrugated roofs, the rest being concrete. Chrysotile is the least harmful of the three asbestos types used for building work. The roof had to be removed and the dust and pieces hosed with water to control any release of fibres to the air. The pieces were placed in bags for disposal and the bags labelled as containing white asbestos.

The insured had its own analytical laboratory which enabled them to determine if stored medicines were usable or should be disposed. At that time, the company was investigating the possibility of moving much of the production to China. So, after removing the asbestos and disposing of it safely, any move to China took over any further interest in a reduced Sydney plant. Therefore no further investigations were needed from us.

Don't Look Down

I have been to Sydney many times and always enjoyed my visits. I was particularly interested in the Sydney Harbour Bridge, built by Dorman Long, the well-known firm of British bridge builders.

So I decided I would book a climb of the bridge. On the appointed day I arrived at the office and the first thing I had to undergo was to be breathalysed. If you have had alcohol in you, you were ruled out immediately.

You are then shown a film of the building of the bridge, after which you are allocated a locker for your clothes and valuables. For safety reasons, you have to wear special thick clothing with no pockets, and you are not allowed to take anything of your own, not even a handkerchief. You also have to wear a very stout belt to which everything is attached on lanyards. This includes a hat, handkerchief, gloves and a radio. It is very cold and windy at the top and you cannot talk to each other, so you stay in contact with the team leader by radio. All the way along the climb, you are attached to a static line to keep you safe and to avoid people trying to end it all by jumping over the edge. You were not able to take a camera, but the leader would take a group photo at the top and an individual shot halfway up.

The bridge has two railway tracks at one side, three lanes of traffic down the middle, and at the right side, both a cycle and a pedestrian lane. The climb is not for the fainthearted. The first part is under the approach to the main bridge. It shakes like mad when a train passes over it, which is very disconcerting. At the end of this section, you then have to climb up a vertical ladder. Once up the ladder, you start the climb up the main bridge. You cannot see down as the floor is solid steel and wide enough to drive a car up it. The climb gets easier as you progress, as the angle to the horizontal decreases as you go upwards.

During the climb you are told about the bridge's construction. About six million rivets were used. Firstly the rivets were heated to red hot, then someone picked up the hot rivets with tongs and presented them to the holes. Finally, the third person hit home the rivets. No protective clothing was provided and the idea of hard hats was unknown in those days. Some people were badly hurt when they were hit on the back of the head by red-hot rivets. The sale of bowler hats increased as people bought these as head protection.

Halfway up Sydney Harbour Bridge

Top of Sydney Harbour Bridge

One of the people who hit home a red-hot rivet lost his balance and fell 400 feet into the harbour below. However, he lived to tell the tale as his heavy hammer overtook him and hit the water first, breaking the surface. If it had not done that, the surface of the water would have been like concrete. He survived but was off work for four weeks with a broken rib. Dorman Long bought him a new hammer.

The bridge was constructed from both ends simultaneously. Each end was secured to rocks. When the two halves finally met in the middle, the workers went off to celebrate with a party lasting for several days. Their celebration was slightly premature. When they returned to work, there was a gap between the two halves of about a metre. This had been caused by temperature changes, which had allowed the halves to expand and contract, resulting in the gap. Ropes securing the two sections had to be slackened off so the gap was removed.

About 13 people lost their lives during construction of the bridge, half of these were on dry land and were killed when a hawser under great tension snapped. This death toll was less than those killed during the building of the English Channel tunnel many years later, despite modern security measures being in place and protective clothing being compulsory.

The Sydney Harbour bridge was opened in 1932. The premier of New South Wales, Jack Lang, was preparing to cut the ribbon when a man in military uniform suddenly appeared on a horse. He galloped across the bridge with a sword and cut the tape, declaring the bridge open. The interloper, called Francis De Groot, declared it open in the name of the New Guard, a right-wing party. He was duly arrested and fined £5 for trespass.

The volume of traffic has built up over the years and the bridge now has a tunnel underneath. One of the bridge's uprights serves as a ventilation shaft for the tunnel.

On the Tourist Trail

Queen Victoria Building

Sydney has plenty of attractions for visitors to enjoy, both inside the city and beyond. There are many trips that can be made by ferries from Circular Quay. To the south you will find pleasant beaches with safe swimming and which are less crowded than places like Bondi.

In the city centre, the Queen Victoria Building (QVB) is pretty impressive.

Dating from the late 19th century, the building occupies a whole block, bounded by George Street, Market Street, York Street and Druitt Street. Originally a market place where goods were bought and sold, it is now a shopping centre and is owned by the city of Sydney. The building was renovated to bring it up to date in 1917, 1933 and 1979. A number of well-known shops selling Australian goods are tenants in the QVB, including Haigh's Chocolates, XXXX Beer, R.M.Williams, Qantas, Speedos and British Airways.

On my first-ever visit to Sydney I booked in to my hotel and went to find a bar to have an after-dinner drink. There was one near the hotel and it was almost empty. The barman came to take my order. I said I would like a pint of Fosters.

'We do not serve those pommy measures and we do not serve Fosters, we send that muck to you poms in the UK,' said the barman. 'I will sell you a schooner of XXXX.'

There was a man sitting near me and he asked if I was from Sydneyside as he had not seen me in the bar before. I said I was from further north. 'Brizzie (Brisbane)?' he asked.

'No,' I said, 'further north.'

'You must be from Darwin.'

'No, further north.'

'But there is nowhere further north,' he said.

'I am from London,' I told him.

'Streuth mate, you are a bloody pom! Have a drink. We then had drinks well into the night. I had made my first Aussie friend in their country. We met up for a few evenings running.

The Rocks area of the city is situated at the end of George Street and not far from the Sydney Harbour Bridge. At weekends the road is closed and a market is held. It is really a tourist trap with souvenir stalls, bars and hotels which are well frequented.

There is a narrow passage from George Street to Cumberland Terrace, which is known as the Suez Canal. You get a good view of the bridge from the top of it. There is a well-known bar near the Rocks called the Fortunes of War. It is reputed to be the oldest pub in Australia and it has quite a history. There was a famous

Australian Rugby Union player, David Campese, who had a shop opposite the pub and if you ever wanted to speak or meet with him, you knew where to find him every lunch time.

If you went up the hill to Cumberland Place, you would come to the George V gym and health club, which was well equipped and well run. I was a regular visitor whenever I was in Sydney. On one occasion I went into the men's changing room, which was usually empty, to find it full. A USA navy ship was at anchor and all the people in there were young Naval Cadets and clearly very fit. When they realised I was from the UK they became very interested in me, asking me questions about Britain, which was on their itinerary on their way home.

Melbourne and Adelaide

James Cook's Cottage

Although I have been to Melbourne more than once, I have never particularly liked this city. To me, it seemed to have a complex about having to play second fiddle to Sydney. It is said to experience four seasons in one day as the weather can be very changeable. It has its good points, however, being more of a centre for the arts than Sydney and it kept its trams, which is a great bonus.

There is also a little gem in the Fitzroy Gardens that's worth a look. Cook's

Cottage was originally built in 1755 in the village of Great Ayton in North Yorkshire. It belonged to James and Grace Cook, the parents of the famous navigator Captain James Cook, who had a very eventful life and was revered in Australia and New Zealand. The cottage was shipped to Melbourne in 1934 and reassembled in Fitzroy Gardens.

Adelaide is a very interesting city and the capital of South Australia. It is said that the city is famous for being full of churches and old people. When I first went there, I was looking for possible places to live in Australia, but I realised I needed somewhere with a little more life. It is nice to visit, but I wasn't ready to join the old folk. The locals will tell that it is the only state not to have taken in migrants. The saying is, 'My forebears arrive with a suitcase and not a criminal record.' When I was there, Adelaide had very few tall buildings, so there are no real skyscrapers.

The Author on the Yarra River

The city is connected to Glen Elg, its seaside town, by a tram service. On my first visit, the trams were old, dating from about 1920. At that time this was the only tram service existing, as all the other lines had been scrapped. On my last visit about three years ago, all the trams had been replaced by modern German ones and the line extended both ways along North Terrace. One old tram has been kept for special occasions.

One hour away from Adelaide is the Murray, Australia's longest river. I spent two days sailing along a tiny part of it, aboard the Murray Princess river boat. After World War Two, someone introduced carp into the river. This fish breeds very quickly and, being a bottom feeder, stirs up the mud. It also kills off the natural species. Various attempts have been made to eliminate it, but without much success. It was a most interesting two days on this mighty river, amid some spectacular scenery.

Tram in Adelaide

Murray Boat

Aussie Efficiency

I liked Australia so much that, as I approached retirement, I decided to buy a property there. The idea was to keep my base in London and then spend a summer in each hemisphere. After much thought about where to live, I settled on the vibrant, fast-growing city of Brisbane. One of the conditions of obtaining a retirement visa to live in Australia was that I had to take out private medical insurance so that I was not a burden on the country. I applied to a medical centre to be taken on to their books. It was only a short drive from where I was living in Brisbane. The set-up was extremely impressive. There was a large basement parking area, with a lift to all floors.

The ground floor consisted of a check-in desk, a waiting area, a newsagent and a pharmacy. The desk had a notice saying, 'If you are kept waiting more than 15 minutes let us know.' Doctors' consulting rooms were located on the first floor. Other floors housed x-ray, MRI and other equipment, massage, acupuncture, osteopathy and physiotherapy. Each of these activities were private companies,

On my first visit I saw my doctor who said I should have an x-ray of my knee. He picked up the telephone and arranged for me to go to have this done. After a 10-minute wait, I had the x-ray and then returned to the waiting area. After 10 minutes I was summoned back by the doctor, who had the results, and by the pharmacy, who had the ointment for me to collect.

The whole procedure took about an hour. I think we could learn much in the UK from Australia and other countries on how run their state medical systems. In London you see your GP who wants tests carried out. You wait to be given an appointment at a local hospital, which can take weeks, except

if it is an emergency. You may have to wait several weeks for the whole process to be completed. It would be helpful if GPs had x-ray equipment in their surgery. This would cut down the time taken to carry out such procedures (while clearly more important investigations would require a referral to a hospital). Dentists have x-ray equipment in their surgeries, so why can't GPs?

14.

Ceylon

My mother had two brothers who were tea planters in Ceylon. In the early 1930s my mother wanted to marry my father. However her family were not keen on the idea. They thought he was not suitable and she could do much better.

My father was a qualified chemist. My mother's parents did not know the difference between a chemist and a pharmacist and wondered which branch of Boots he served in. Did he live over the shop? The fact that he was half German and half Scottish, didn't work in his favour either. They came up with a plan to send their daughter out to Ceylon to stay with her elder brother, see something of the country and hopefully meet someone more suitable as a husband. She was away for nine months.

My mother enjoyed the sea voyage there. Many of her fellow travellers were not getting off at Colombo, Ceylon's capital, but travelling on to Madras in India. Quite a few of them seemed to be well connected socially. But there was one woman, a Mrs Coward, who was ignored by many of her fellow travellers. She ran a small boarding house near Teddington and her husband was a not very successful piano salesman. Money was scarce in the family home and it was left to her son to be the breadwinner.

My mother liked Mrs Coward and found her very interesting. She was travelling to see her son Eric, who was also a tea planter. My mother asked if he was her only son. She replied, 'No, I have another one who is involved with the theatre.' The penny then dropped. Her son was none other than Noel Coward. Born in 1899, Noel Coward was an actor, playwright, composer, director and singer. By the time he was 20 he had written and performed many popular songs and acted in many plays. He was also popular in the USA. He became rich, had friends in high places, including royalty, and owned houses in Kent, Jamaica and France.

My mother and Mrs Coward got on very well and enjoyed spending time in each other's company. Unfortunately, my mother did not keep contact with Mrs Coward back at home. I often thought of all those first nights she might have been invited to.

When the ship arrived in Colombo my mother was met by her brother Francis and taken to Nuwara Eliya where he was based. There were many single men in Ceylon who, although they were well paid and had houses and servants provided, were very lonely. There were very few single women around. There were many single men living on their own, usually dressed for dinner to keep up appearances. To address this situation, the first marriage bureau was set up in London, the idea being to find suitable girls for single men in Ceylon and it was very successful. There was a similar situation in other countries, such as India. The girls were known as 'the fishing fleet', many of whom were in their late twenties or older and had not found a man back home.

Having heard so much about Ceylon from my mother and uncles, I decided in 1999 to visit the country. I joined a party of travellers and flew to Colombo. We spent the first two nights at Mount Lavinia Hotel, south of the capital. Next day we travelled north to the famous elephant sanctuary. It was originally set up as an orphanage for young ones who have lost their parents. At the sanctuary they are fed, given medical care and are encouraged to mate.

Mount Lavinia

Elephant Orphanage

One of the problems faced there is that wild elephants, seeing what a good time the orphans were having, wanted to join in. Rangers have to dissuade them, since there would not be enough food for all of them. The permanent residents are very friendly, unlike African elephants, and like being scrubbed and fed bananas. I made the great mistake of peeling the bananas first. The elephant threw it on the ground and stamped on it. A mahout said to me they like eating the whole fruit, skins and all.

On another occasion I rode an elephant through a river. When we were nearing the other side, it lowered its trunk into the water, which I could not understand. The trunk then came up, turned around backwards and I suddenly saw what it was about to do. It blew water all over me, soaking me and my passport. Then it gave me a smug smile.

Riding Elephants

We then went down to the south-west corner of the island to a seaside hotel where we enjoyed lovely sunny weather. I wanted to go to Colombo, so I thought I would take the train. I took a taxi to the local station and enquired when the next train would be arriving. I was told by the taxi driver that train drivers were on strike and there would be no trains that day.

A train arrived going south, so clearly not all drivers were on strike. A taxi driver came to me and said that, because of the strike, he would take me in his taxi for a similar price. I decided to find the station master. He said that what the taxi driver had told me was untrue, the trains were running normally and that a taxi ride would be much more expensive. A train arrived after a 10-minute wait. It was packed, except for seats at the front and back of each carriage. A notice on these seats said, 'Reserved for the clergy'. I sat down on one of the seats. A man came up to me and said that those seats were for clergy only. I replied that I would sit there until a member of the clergy needed it. I did not have to give up my seat

Fully Loaded Train

I hired a tuk tuk at the station to take me round the city. Many of the shops looked very old fashioned. I had a good look round and then went to the Galle Face Hotel for lunch. Afterwards I took a taxi back to the station. The train was in but did not have an engine, so it was not going anywhere in a hurry. As much as I looked I could not find a seat. I did not want to stand all the way. I got off the train, wondering when the next train was scheduled.

A young guy came up to me and asked if I was looking for a seat. I said yes, and immediately there was a seat available. I sat down and he asked me to make a donation to an old folks home. I gave him the equivalent of five pounds and he was happy. I had heard about these scams but it was worth it to avoiding standing.

During my trip I decided to visit Nuwara Eliya, the centre of the tea-growing area. I had heard about the Hill Club. First established by British coffee and tea planters, it was the social club for ex-pats, mainly from the tea estates. When I went there, I saw in one of the rooms a list of chairmen over the years. My Uncle Francis, my mother's brother, was listed as being a chairman but he only served for one year. All the others had served for at least two or more years. I thought I would find out why. Apparently, during his time as chairman he brought into the club a very successful business man to have lunch. The man was a person of colour and was not an ex-pat. Members were very annoyed about this and at the end of the year my uncle was not allowed to stand again, though he kept his membership.

Hill Club

I was hoping to visit the city of Trincomalee but that was not possible due to the civil war. The reason I wanted to go was because of my family's connection with it. My uncle Michael, another of my mother's brothers and my godfather, was in the Royal Navy. He was commander in charge of flying on the aircraft carrier HMS Hermes when it received orders from Winston Churchill. The previous week the Japanese had bombed and sank the battleship Prince of Wales and the battlecruiser Repulse with great loss of life. Churchill described this as his worst moment of the war.

At the time Churchill ordered it to sea, HMS Hermes was being refitted in Trincomalee and did not have any aircraft on board. An aircraft carrier's method of defence is its aircraft. It did not even have a spotter plane that could have given early warning. My uncle was on the flight deck at the time of the attack and was killed instantly.

HMS Hermes, An open day in Portsmouth

One of the stories that my mother told me about her brother Michael was the time when, as a young midshipman in the Royal Navy, he had been ordered during the General Strike of 1926 to take a platoon of ratings to the Fulham power station. At the time it was privately owned and needed to be protected because the strikers considered it a prime target. They would, if they could, try to put it out of action. If they managed to cause damage to it, my uncle was ordered to open fire on the strikers. Fortunately this had not been necessary.

My brother David and I met Uncle Michael on two occasions. In 1940 he took us to Hamleys in Regent Street to buy us toys. The second occasion was in 1942 when we were staying with friends of our parents. He had a bandage on his right hand, which had been caused by a piece of schrapnel. David and I asked him to remove the bandage so we could see the wound. He did not oblige. I was very sad when I heard he had been killed. Years later, I took my mother to Dartmouth and Plymouth to see the Royal Navy College and the war memorial.

When I was in Rhodesia, I met a man called Clive Lang, an ex-Royal Navy man, who had also been on HMS Hermes. He had known my uncle well and Michael was his best man in Cape Town at Clive's marriage to Collete, a South African girl. A Japanese bomb blew the side off Hermes and about 30 crew, including Clive, went down with the ship. Miraculously, they all came to the surface on a large air bubble on 23 January 1942.

My Uncle and Godfather in full Naval Dress

15.

In The Club

In 1953 I was taken by a school friend to the Hurlingham Club in West London. I had heard of it but had never visited it. On entering the main gate I was confronted by 44 acres of superb gardens and a Victorian mansion which was now the club house. In 1926 the club decided to buy the house and gardens directly to the east up to Broom House Lane. The house was called Broom House, which was then demolished and the cricket ground was created. Unknowingly, this was a good move due to what was proposed years later, when the council sought a compulsory purchase of the polo grounds.

I met a young architect who said he had just been recruited by the London County Council (LCC) who were planning the takeover of the club premises for building council flats. I said I was planning to apply for membership, but he told me I would be wasting my time, as work would be starting in the next 18 months.

The committee at the time came up with the idea of offering membership to all of Attlees's Labour cabinet. The only person who took up this offer was Ernest Bevin who was foreign secretary and who liked taking Mrs Bevin to the Sunday tea dances. He recommended that the LCC and the local council take over the polo and practice ground, leaving what is now the club's grounds.

The practice ground in Broom House Lane is now covered by council flats. The polo ground is now Hurlingham Park, which was handed to the National Playing Fields Association.

During World War Two, the club allowed local residents to use the polo area for allotments. At the end of the war, the council refused to hand it back.

Apart from having well-kept gardens, the club had about 40 tennis courts. In summer, half of these were grass courts and the others hard. There were also four squash courts, two swimming pools – one outdoor and one indoors – along with a cricket ground, croquet and bowls lawns.

I was 18 at the time I was first shown the club and I thought I must join. To do this I had to be proposed and seconded by existing members. The club secretary showed me a book of members and I realised that I knew a member, but he was the only one. Then I met another member at a drinks party who said he would second me. I completed the paperwork and became a member three weeks later.

There was no entry fee and my annual subscription, being aged under 28, was 13 guineas (13 pounds and 13 shillings). On reaching 28, the fee went up to 15 guineas. I took my parents there and my mother thought she would like to join, which I arranged. A year later I proposed my younger brother John and he also joined with little delay.

I had played tennis badly before I joined, so I decided to have tennis lessons. I first started playing tennis aged 12. My mother was keen that myself and my two brothers should learn to play tennis as soon as we were old enough. It was one of those things that children should learn how to do, not only as a sport but as a social event.

My mother found a coach who gave lessons on a court near Kensington Church

Street. Aged 12, I was entering a rebellious frame of mind and was in no mood to cooperate. Despite the efforts of the coach I was happy to hit every ball either into the net or out of the court. I won this little contest, as the coach complained to my mother that he could do nothing with me. I told my mother that I was happy to leave as I said the man was no good.

I had no such complaints at Hurlingham, where I took lessons with Mr Jeffery, the senior coach. I made such good progress that I decided to play in doubles games. I also made good use of the club's swimming pools and regular social events. There wasn't a gym in those days. During winter, I was a regular at Highland dancing classes. This proved useful when working abroad in Johannesburg and also in the British Embassy in Yemen. Naturally, it was also an asset during visits to Scotland.

I had two spells as an overseas member when working in Southern Rhodesia and in South Africa. In total, I have been a member for approaching 70 years. This must make me one of the longest serving members. With this in mind, I asked the membership office to let me know where I am in the longevity pecking order. Apparently I am tenth out of 6,000 full members.

During my time I have seen the rebuilding of the East Wing, a new outside swimming pool, the replacement of the tea servery, new indoor courts for tennis and squash, the rebuilding of the tennis pavilion after the fire, and the building of a gym. I have also been amazed at the expensive fiasco of the attempt for a total rebuild of the west wing.

Although I can no longer take part in sporting activities, on fine days I do visit the Club on my electric scooter. Over the years, Hurlingham has been an oasis which I can visit easily as I live nearby.

One of the benefits of being a member is that Hurlingham has reciprocity with clubs overseas. I have visited clubs in Australia, (Adelaide, Melbourne, Perth, Sydney), New Zealand, (Auckland, Christchurch, Wellington), Singapore, South Africa (Cape Town, Johannesburg). Those in the UK include, in London, Caledonian, Carlton, City Club and East India.

Hurlingham

The Polo ground during The War

Marylebone Cricket Club

A cousin of my mother's was a keen member of the MCC and he suggested that he propose my two brothers for membership. For some reason he was convinced that I was not interested, which was not true. I was so annoyed that I asked my house master at Wellington whether he would propose me, which he did. My father had a friend who was an MCC member who said he would second me.

At that time they were rebuilding the Warner Stand and the committee were looking at ways of paying for it. They decided on introducing a category of Associate Membership for young members. I was duly elected and a year or two later I became a full member. Some years later this cousin of my mother's said to me, 'You must be very grateful to me for getting you into the MCC'. I told him that I was not grateful since he refused to propose me, which I resent to this day.

Members' Pavilion

Institute of Directors

The Institute was founded in 1903 and incorporated by Royal Charter in 1906. According to its mission statement, it stands for free enterprise, entrepreneurism, wealth creation and good corporate governance.

I first came across it when it was located in Belgrave Square where it occupied two buildings. It is now located at 116 Pall Mall. The site is part of the Royal Estate and was previously occupied by the United Service Club, known as the 'Senior'. This was for senior officers in the Royal Navy and British Army above the rank of commander or major. It closed in 1978.

The IOD had been looking for larger premises and 116 Pall Mall proved to be ideal. The building had to be completely refurbished and bedrooms removed. One of the conditions was that all traditional painting had to remain.

An Australian member who lived in the same building as me was a keen member and encouraged me to join. Her family firm of engineers had tendered to build the Sydney Harbour Bridge and was shortlisted. In the end the contract was awarded to Dorman Long, the famous firm of bridge builders. The reason why they were awarded the contract was that much of the sub-assemblies would be made on site and not brought in from abroad. She invited me to the annual IOD lunch at the Royal Albert Hall. Sir Roy Walensky, Prime Minister of the Federation of Rhodesia and Nyasaland, was the guest of honour and my Australian friend thought, quite rightly, that I would be interested. Walensky described himself as being half Polish, half Jewish and 100 per cent British. His first job in North Rhodesia was with the railways, driving steam locomotives.

Sir Roy was one of the principal speakers at the lunch and it was his speech that convinced me I should emigrate to the Federation.

In 2021 I have reached the age of 86 having been a member of the IOD for about 60 years. During that time I have enjoyed my membership and have learnt a lot. I wish them continued success in future.

The Commonwealth Schools Club (CSC)

The CSC was set up Salisbury, Rhodesia, as a sports and social club. The founding fathers had wanted to call it the Public Schools Club. However, Prime Minister Sir Roy Walensky was keen to join, but he had not been to a public school in the English sense. The name, therefore, became the Commonwealth Schools Club.

I was taken to the CSC by a friend and immediately applied to join. It had been started with little money but as membership grew, improvements were made. It had a club house and four tennis courts but little else. It was open every evening and all days at weekends and public holidays. The bar and cafe were the main sources of income. I made many friends there, some of whom remained friends after my eventual return to the UK.

The club's 'staff' consisted of members who manned the bar, cooked and served the food and cleaned the club house. At that time there was not enough money to recruit paid staff. Friday evenings were the most popular and much drink was consumed. At 7pm they had a bonsella (a gift). Each member was given a number. A sum of money was put into a kitty and if the owner of the number was present, he or she could claim the bonsella. If not present, the money would remain and be added to the following week, I think it was about £30 each week. As the amount increased, more people would visit the club. Hence drink sales covered the cost of the bonsella. Once it reached about £100 or more, the club was crowded and club funds benefitted.

Maurice, an Irish friend of mine, and I would often meet for dinner in the evening. After one evening he suggested we went to the Venus Room in Frith Street. I did not know what to expect.

At the time, theatres were badly hit by television. To counter this, theatres had introduced nude shows but the girls were not allowed to move. Strip clubs were then set up to counter this. If it was a members' club, the performers were allowed to move. Apart from their heads, the girls were shaved of all body hair. I paid a small sum and was given life membership. The performers would come on and strip to an old record played on an even older record player.

At the end of one performance I bought a girl a drink and had a long talk to her. She had been a typist in her previous job, earning £4.50 per week. She was doing this job to earn sufficient money to buy a flat or small house. She recognised that it would take her about three years to earn sufficient to reach her target. I wished her well.

I heard later that Westminster City Council had closed the club for keeping a disorderly house (brothel). Although I was a life member, it was not my lifetime but that of the club.

Australia

The Adelaide Club

I went to live in Australia for six months of the year. I have always suffered from the cold and it seemed to me to be a good idea to have summer there and then come back to UK for the English summer. I did this for about eight years running and it worked well.

I had been to Australia when I was working. I liked Sydney but it was a very expensive place to buy property. I also like Adelaide and Brisbane. Someone told me that Adelaide was full of old people and churches. As nice as it was, I did not feel that I was ready to join them.

The Adelaide Club had a policy of not having any women members. Wives of members could stay, but had to enter via the side (servants') door and go up immediately to their room. They were not allowed to use the public rooms and bar. On my first visit, I had lunch with the club secretary. I asked him why they did not have lady members. 'We are not going down that path like you people in Britain' was his reply.

I had reciprocity with the club from the Hurlingham Club in London. I visited it on a number of occasions when travelling between Australia and London. On one such visit, I was meeting a friend, Pauline, who was also a member of Hurlingham in London. We had arranged to meet in the bar at 12 noon. I had forgotten that women were not allowed there. We therefore had to go to a neighbouring bar to have a drink and something to eat. The last time I stayed in the Adelaide Club the rules had been changed. Women could now use the bar if accompanied by a member.

The Brisbane Club

Brisbane had a real buzz about it and was the fastest developing part of the Commonwealth of Australia. I bought a unit (flat) in a new development, which I thoroughly enjoyed and could let when back in London.

The Brisbane Club was housed in the city centre in a new office block called Brisbane Chambers. It occupied the basement, plus floors two, three and four. It was largely for business people and, after I had been vetted by the committee, I was also admitted. Although lacking the facilities of other clubs, such as accommodation, they concentrated on providing good food and wine. From my point of view it was a good place to meet people and to entertain friends from Britain.

The club had themed lunches on the top floor which were always worthwhile. On many occasions wine growers would present their new wines for tasting. On another occasion, the French Ambassador talked to us about the benefits of the European Union. You could also hire the room for private parties.

In Sydney, a Hurlingham member could use The Royal Sydney Golf Club and also the Union University and Schools Club. I had dinner at the Union University Club but was not impressed.

16.

Italy

My first visit to Italy took place in 1959. I had recently left University and had never travelled abroad. The scientific consultancy I worked for had a client who imported concentrated orange juice into the UK. Their buyer had reported that their juice had been adulterated. The practice in those days was to concentrate orange juice by taking out water so that it became six times more concentrated. The buyer in the UK would then put back the water so that it was the same as fresh juice.

The contents of the juice were easily measured using a refractometer. This pocket-sized meter gives a reading, known as Brix, showing the amount of soluble solids in the juice. This is nearly all sugars. Hence a six-times concentrated juice would show a Brix of six. The offending juice had a figure of six, but chemical analysis showed the sugars present were not sucrose (normal sugar), but invert sugar formed by the acid hydrolysis of a starchy material. Crucially, invert sugar is very cheap, so a mixture with orange juice could be passed off as the real thing since it showed the correct Brix. The adulterated juice would look the same and taste the same. It was being passed off as the real thing and hence charged the normal price, but was made from much cheaper ingredients and hence gave a greater profit.

I had to get to Messina in Sicily. I flew from London to Rome by Air Italia and then took the sleeper train down to Reggio in the south of Italy. The whole train, less locomotive, was put on the ferry three carriages at a time.

In Messina, I was based in a Joly Hotel. I was taken out to the factory and shown the whole method of extracting juice. I was very interested to see what else they were doing, but they were not making concentrate that day. They were extracting juice from fruit.

The next day they were not making concentrate either, so I was taken on a sightseeing tour of the east coast. I went to Catania to see another plant that was doing nothing. Then to Taormina, a beautiful spot which I thought I would visit in the future.

On the following day I was taken out by a charming German who was their chief salesman. I was told there was a problem in the factory, which would take a few days to correct. I was then taken to see Mount Etna and a general trip round.

Back in Messina I was getting very suspicious. I bought a newspaper and saw an article about how many people were producing adulterated products, which had nearly killed the trade. The article said that prosecutions would soon follow. Citrus products were one of the main industrial products on the island, and hence its loss was causing financial harm and loss of jobs.

I felt I had failed to solve the problem facing UK buyers. There was little I could do as I was being prevented from seeing any production. I took the train back to Rome and then took a taxi for a quick tour of the city. I changed my flight back to London, taking a later one back to the UK.

A few years later a friend had recently bought a Morris Minor car, which had just been launched on to the market. He was planning to take a holiday in it, driving to Italy and asked me if I would like to come too. It was easy to say yes. We set off, crossing the English Channel by ferry and then drove through France, stopping at pensions along the way. After France we drove into Switzerland, where we both managed to contract food poisoning. The best way to combat food poisoning was to be the driver. The brain has much to do when you are the driving, so you cannot feel ill and drive at the same time. When one of us felt ill, we took the wheel.

Then into Italy. Apart from my brief stay in Rome, I had not been to mainland

Italy before. It was nice to see the lakes of Maggiore, Orta, Garda and Como. We then drove to Milan, keeping to the ringroad heading for Verona. We decided to go to the Verona festival in the evening to see some opera. Unfortunately, the opera was being staged in an old Roman open-air theatre very near the airport. Much of the singing was being drowned out by low-flying aircraft. We decided to try again the next afternoon when there were fewer aircraft landing. We heard the Barber of Seville.

On the way back, we decided to see the Cinque Terra by boat in both directions, leaving the car at the starting point. We had an uneventful, nausea-free journey back to the UK.

The last job I did as consultant for an American firm of loss adjusters, I was asked to fly as soon as possible to a factory south of Turin, which produced toilet rolls. I flew on a Sunday afternoon to Turin and picked up a left-hand drive diesel hire car to drive south to the factory. The journey was one of the worst I have even driven. Trying to leave the airport, I could not get the car to start as I had never driven a diesel car before. After receiving help I finally set off. The first part of the journey was on the ringroad around Turin. The drivers all seemed to me to be maniacs, getting annoyed with me driving in the middle lane of three and overtaking me on both sides. We then had a torrential downpour with which the windscreen wipers could not cope.

I decided to pull over on to the hard shoulder to let the storm pass over. The next thing I knew, a police car had parked behind me and said I was breaking the law by stopping on the hard shoulder. They told me to drive on. I had to, keeping to a slow speed and was then hooted by following cars because they thought I was too slow.

I then came to a payage. There were three booths where you could pay and I chose the one with the least vehicles. What I did not know was it was for heavy vehicles only. I was now hemmed in. No one would let me out. I did not have GB plates, so they assumed I was a local trying to queue barge. I did get out eventually, but had to join one of the other queues, which was now much longer than when I had arrived at the payage.

Fortunately the rain stopped and I came to the side road where I had to turn off.

There were no sign posts and I got lost trying to find the village where I would be staying. It took one hour to find the right village and then the hotel. I arrived in the nick of time. The hotel said that, as I had not arrived, they assumed that I was not coming after all. They were about to let the room to someone else.

I found the factory next day and was shown around by the factory manager. He was very unpleasant and spent most of the time swearing at his young assistant.

The factory itself was similar to another in the same group, in Barrow-in-Furness, North-West England, that I had investigated quite recently. In both cases a warehouse had been destroyed by fire. My job was to ascertain the amount of stock affected by smoke in the warehouse, where the fire had started, and in adjoining warehouses. We had a series of meetings arranged by the factory manager. He had asked some people, such as accountants, to attend, who had nothing to do with assessing the extent of damage.

I set out what I intended to do. I would assess the extent of the damage in neighbouring warehouses, to rule out those unaffected. Stock in the affected warehouse was also examined and smoke-damaged stock identified by smell. The nose is very sensitive, but after about 30 minutes needs to be resensitised by fresh air. For that reason, the assessment is best done by a team that takes it in turns to assess stock.

I felt very sorry for the manager's assistant. Jobs were very scarce in the area and this was the only job he could get. But his real interest was in the arts. I wished him well and suggested he should try to change jobs because working for that manager was not doing him any good. Fortunately my drive back to Turin went without a hitch.

On another occasion I visited the Vatican, which was very interesting. I was, however, surprised when taking the lift to the top, with the 12 apostles nearby, to be confronted with a Coca Cola dispenser. Nevertheless, there was a sense of peace and relaxation in the whole Vatican City.

My only other visit to Italy was on two occasions to Madesimo for skiing holidays, where I twice did the Canalone. This a very long run, not all that difficult, but very tiring.

17.

Accommodation

I was the first of the three brothers to leave home in the late 1950s. I contacted a firm called 'Share a Flat' who specialised in finding accommodation for young people of similar backgrounds. I moved into a flatshare in South Kensington with two double bedrooms and a large sitting room, each paying £3 per week. Fortunately, we housemates all got on well and we even played cupid for one of them. We held a party in the flat and I invited some friends, who included a female cousin of mine. The party went well and one of the other flat sharers hit it off with my cousin. Some time later, I heard they were engaged to be married.

My brother John was the next to go and he went into a more spacious flat in Notting Hill, but he had to share with five other guys. In those days you did not mix the sexes when flat sharing. This left my elder brother David still living with the parents. He thought his time had come and that he, too, should leave home. He knew a rather eccentric peer of the realm from his days in the army doing National Service. The peer had his own flat in South Kensington and was looking for a tenant. David saw the flat. It was large and well furnished, so he decided to move in.

All went well in the first two weeks, but then his lordship decided to buy a small monkey. He said it was not a problem, as there was a spare bedroom that the monkey could use. After a while, the monkey got bored and decided he would leave his room. He liked climbing up the curtains in the drawing room and sitting on top of the pelmet and relieving himself.

At that time his lordship and his monkey drove around London in a Morris minivan which had no windows in the back, but a ventilator in the roof. David, meanwhile, was a junior barrister based in the Temple and he travelled to work on the District Line. He went to take the train back from Temple to South Kensington but was told that there had been an incident and trains were suspended. He then had to take a series of buses to reach South Kensington.

When he eventually reached his flat there was a real crisis. The monkey had escaped from the van. He had managed to dismantle the ventilator and escaped through the hole in the roof. My brother then heard on the radio that District line trains had been suspended due a monkey, which had been spotted sitting on one of the electrified lines.

When he got back to the flat, there were a number of services outside, including an ambulance, the police and the RSPCA. The fire brigade had also been summoned. The monkey was somewhere in the nearby underground. The RSPCA produced some nets, but they did not extend up to the roof of the tunnel and the monkey just jumped over it. After a while they admitted defeat and withdrew. In the end, London Zoo suggested that some food was left at a convenient place as, after a few hours, hunger would take over. They also agreed to give a home to the animal.

Apart from being fined for keeping a wild animal in a private residence, my brother's friend was ordered to remove it. London Transport put in a claim for loss of revenue and inconvenience to the general public. The police, fire brigade and RSPCA also wanted compensation for their efforts. By this point my brother had had enough and he asked my parents whether he could move back in. After that troubling experience, David continued to live at home until he married.

Augusto & Aida Caprani

The Port at Split

The Palace of Diocletian

Cheap and Not So Cheerful

In 1961, I decided to rent a furnished flat with a Cambridge friend of mine. His mother had heard of a flat in Knightsbridge in Old Barrack Yard near Hyde Park Corner. We both went to look at it on a Sunday afternoon. It was the upper floor of what would have been the stables to a larger house. It had two good-sized bedrooms and an open-plan living area. You could get to it from Old Barrack Yard off Knightsbridge Road, or from Wilton Place.

Our landlord was the Savoy Hotel Group and the rent was very low. This was because the Group was buying the properties in order to build a new Berkeley Hotel, located in Berkeley Square. Our contract was on the basis that, when the time came, we would vacate the premises within two weeks. There would be no charges for reparations or repainting as the building was due for demolition.

We soon realised why we had been shown the flat on a Sunday afternoon. Next door was a nightclub called Esmeralda's Barn. It was run by the Kray twins and it operated between 9pm and 3am. The noise from music, people shouting and vibration made sleep impossible.

The Kray twins were not people you could argue with. Barbara Windsor, a friend of theirs, was a frequent visitor. On another occasion I recognised Lord Boothby there, too. He had been a cabinet minister in the Conservative government, but was too outspoken and made many enemies. He also became friends with the Krays.

The flat was overrun with cockroaches. Coming back after work, my first job was to collect about 100 and put them down the toilet. There was a courtyard at ground-floor level, which contained overflowing rubbish bins and there were rats everywhere. Customers from Esmeralda's used the bins for urinating and to be sick, often dropping the metal lids onto the ground. Others who did not make it in time were sick on the ground. The smell was appalling.

I was hoping that council inspectors would shut down the whole area due to risks to public health. I began to wonder if their non-appearance was due to fright, or cash-filled brown envelopes. One day two policemen were in the yard. I thought they had come to investigate the area. Unfortunately this was not the case. They took off their helmets, pulled out their cigarettes and lit up. I realised that they were not there to investigate conditions, but to enjoy the skive point on their beat.

On leaving the flat by the Wilton Place entrance, you passed a series of studios. The first took photos of naked men and women. I had no idea there was a market for this. The next one catered for body builders and the door was usually left open. They all seemed to be dressed in jock straps. One asked me if I would like to look round, which I refused. 'You now know where to come if you want any photos taken,' he told me. I thanked him and said I would that bear that in mind, but did not take up the offer.

My parents wanted to see where I was living. Understandably, I was not keen on the idea and put them off on many occasions. Eventually they turned up unannounced and were horrified. My mother said that the only thing good about it was it had a Belgravia telephone number.

From our point of view, the second good point was that the Grenadier pub was not far away, where we could have a drink and a good meal away from the madhouse of Old Barrack Yard.

I put up with it for about four months then, since I was planning to go and live in Rhodesia,

I went and lived back at home for two months before setting off. The site is now occupied by the New Berkeley, a very much upmarket hotel, which has raised the tone of the area.

A London Madhouse

On my return from Africa I needed somewhere to live so I returned to 'Share a Flat'. They advertised that they took great pains to match up people of similar backgrounds and interests.

They found me a flat in South Kensington to share with two other guys. Astrologer Russell Grant lived above in the top-floor flat and had a succession of clients visiting him most days.

My new flatmate Bill was an out-of-work accountant who could not find a job, despite the demand for his profession. When I looked at his CV I realised why. Apart from his basic details, his résumé was basically a list of his medical aliments. I re-wrote it for him and within a week he had obtained a job with Tarmac.

The other guy had a good job but wanted to chuck it in and become a landscape architect. He had a girlfriend and they were planning to get married. After a short while the girlfriend moved in. She did not work and spent nearly all her time in the flat, leaving the central heating on all day. I suggested that she contribute to the cost of running the flat, which they both refused. In the end they gave up and moved out.

A few weeks later I heard that Bill was in hospital, seriously ill with cancer. I went to see him but he looked much the same. On my next visit he looked almost unrecognisable and really ill. He died a few weeks later. I was sorry I had ignored his continual grumbling about his aches and pains. I thought he was one of those people who liked to talk about their ailments. I did not think he had anything serious to complain about. We replaced Bill with a guy whose family had just returned from Kenya and wanted somewhere to stay in London. The would-be landscape architect, having left, had created another vacancy. I was going to be out of London on a consulting assignment for three weeks so I told the guy from Kenya to find a suitable replacement.

'Share a Flat' sent an Old Etonian. When I returned from my trip I met him and was surprised to discover that his name was Baron Clement Franckenstein. His father had been the Austrian ambassador to Great Britain at the time Hitler had taken over Austria. He had become friendly with King George VI, who agreed to be young Clement's godfather.

Eton-educated Clement was not what I expected. He had shoulder-length hair, looked unwashed

and had a large sexual appetite. More than once I came in from work to find him lying on the drawing-room floor in flagrante with a young girl, not always the same one. I told him to use his bedroom and not the drawing room floor in future.

Clement had a Minivan, which he drove around London unlicensed, uninsured and minus an MOT certificate. More than once the police arrived looking for him. He had ignored summons and they had a warrant for his arrest. He often returned in the early hours of the morning. He was involved with a nightclub and also helped in managing a pop group.

I saw later in the Daily Mail that Franckenstein had moved to Hollywood, leaving a trail of debts, to try to break into pictures. The Mail reported that, 'Fangs are not what they used to be for Baron Franckinstein'. However, he did manage to secure a stream of small parts in films. He died in 1974 in Los Angeles.

I had just bought a small furniture making firm in High Wycombe and planned to move out of London. It was a treat to get away, finally, from the London madhouse.

Home Improvements

During the 1970s I bought a terraced house in Fulham, West London. It was typical of houses built around 1900 and consisted of three rooms downstairs and two upstairs. There was no bathroom and the only toilet it had was outside. One of the attractions was that it had a good-sized garden, which was totally overgrown.

Overall, the house was in a terrible state with gas, water, windows and electrics in need of replacing. I paid £35,000 for it and set about bringing it up to date. Fortunately I had been able to save money, but I still needed to take out a mortgage of £14,000 to meet the full figure.

My father came to see what I had bought. I showed him around in silence and asked him what he thought. 'I think you have taken leave of your senses,' was his uncompromising verdict. My mother said the house was typical of where her domestic servants would come from.

The third room downstairs contained a large range used for cooking and providing heat. All the other rooms had open fireplaces for heating. The first thing to go was the range and its huge chimney, which extended into the middle bedroom upstairs and up through the roof into the open air.

There was now a problem. The chimney was attached to the neighbour's chimney and therefore removal posed a real problem. A compromise was reached. Steel brackets were cemented into the wall to take the weight of my part of the double chimney. Problem sorted, a passage could now be created, giving me a third bedroom. Over a 10-year period I created a very pleasant residence, with the help of an excellent builder

When I had my house in Fulham I got to know some of my neighbours, including an Italian couple, who became close friends. The husband was in the catering business and had to work long shifts,

while his wife worked for a large chain of retail shops. They both had to work hard and were good at their respective businesses.

The time came for them to retire. They sold up and went to live in Italy. They also bought a holiday apartment in Split in Croatia. They kept in contact with me and have invited me to stay with them in Split on many occasions.

Croatia was previously part of Yugoslavia. It now thrives as a very popular holiday resort. It has excellent weather in summer and mild winters. It is a lot cheaper and less crowded than Italy, with a population of about four million.

The city of Split has parts that have a heritage going back to Roman times. Some of the houses on the seafront were built by the Romans and are still inhabited today. The main market is in a Roman-built building, while the Roman aqueduct is still bringing water to the city.

Split is one of largest traders with the European Union which, along with tourism and agriculture, makes it is a prosperous country. The airport in Split was small but, as the tourist trade increased, it proved to be totally inadequate. Fortunately, a new terminal building has been constructed to solve the problem. A number of cruise ships call in regularly.

One of a Kind

In 1976 I was looking for somewhere to live in London and heard from a friend that a school headmistress had bought a three-bedroom flat in Kensington for her retirement. During the war she had worked at Bletchley Park code-breaking station. She wanted to let the flat to two young people of the right type who would cover the outgoings, which amounted to £12 per week. She wanted the small third bedroom kept for her use when in London, which was about four times per year.

I knew a man who was also looking for somewhere to live in London. We seemed to go to the same parties. He was very friendly to everyone, whether you were well educated, or a dustman, road sweeper or postman. His name was Andrew Keith. He had played rugby for Rugby School, was an excellent squash player and had played in Junior Wimbledon. Women found him very attractive.

Andrew had been a master at Gordonstoun, teaching French and German. However, when Prince Charles started going to the school they got rid of all the unqualified teachers, including Andrew. He had always been interested in antiques, something his mother had taught him. He took a job with an auction house, as a porter, which is a good way to start. His father was Scottish and had been in the Royal Navy. Coincidentally, his father had also worked at Bletchley Park like our landlady, the school headmistress, whom he met during the time Andrew lived in the flat. The father was a bit of a martinet and was very strict with Andrew and his elder brother Peter. Unfortunately, Peter was drowned when swimming in Spain, where his uncle and aunt had taken him as a reward for having won a scholarship to Cambridge.

Andrew joined the flat and we got on very well. Unfortunately, time meant nothing to him and he was always late for everything. My brother John and I had told my parents that Andrew was very friendly, generous and a kind person. He also liked the ladies and usually got his wicked way. My parents were coming up to

London to attend some function and decided to visit Andrew and me in the flat. My mother was horrified by what she had heard about him and said she would wear gloves in case he wanted to shake hands. 'You never know where those little hands have been,' she said.

When my parents arrived Andrew was absolutely charming and immediately won them over. He had prepared drinks, which we all enjoyed. My father liked him immediately and my mother accused me of making up the stories about him that were obviously untrue.

Andrew Keith

He then joined Richard Green, who had two art galleries in Dover Street. Andrew was very successful with clients and good at charming potential clients. Green's Uncle Henry was taken on to run a second gallery in Dover Street. He had been a second-hand car dealer and whilst he had the chat, he knew nothing about antique pictures. Andrew was given the job of working in this second gallery to provide the relevant knowledge to make the gallery a success. Andrew and Uncle Henry became firm friends and they both liked their drink. Andrew also became friends with Bing Crosby, who was a frequent visitor to the main gallery. They would meet up whenever Bing was in London.

Andrew's mother was English and extremely rich. When she died, Andrew was left millions of pounds and land in Hampshire. Unfortunately this was his downfall. He always had a liking for drink but now he took to heavy drinking. He lost his job with Richard Green after he started arriving late for work, stinking of drink and sales were suffering. He also lost his driving licence after being breathalysed.

The money left to Andrew was huge and estimates put it between five and 15 million pounds. When he died there was little left. Apart from drink he wasted money on buying stakes in two racehorses. He never saw the horses but he kept getting demands for payment for stable and trainer's fees. I began to wonder if the horses ever existed. It could have easily been a successful scam. He asked to see the horses on one occasion, but was told they had picked up a virus and had to be put down.

He also liked eating out at expensive restaurants and tipping lavishly. On a trip to Hong Kong, he ordered four suits, six blazers and 24 shirts from a tailor. Most of these he never seemed to wear. He travelled often by air, usually first class.

He went to the 2000 Olympic Games in Australia, having bought a season ticket for many thousands of dollars, but only went there once since no one was allowed to drink there. For the rest of the games, he watched it on TV in his Sydney hotel room so that he could drink.

Another expensive waste of money was a Mercedes sports car, which he could not drive as he had lost his licence. It was left rusting outside his house and, having paid thousands of pounds for it, he sold it for £200.

His death was a shock to his many friends but we all knew that heavy drinking would get him in the end. I went to his funeral and gave the farewell speech. I had been told by a friend, who was a parson, to keep it light. I started my speech by saying, ' I am going to talk about the Screwings and Doings of Andrew.' Fortunately it went down well and the officiating priest said to me at the end of the service he had never heard so much laughter at a funeral before. Andrew was 61 years old when he died. Money does not bring happiness but it can oil the wheels.

18.

Contaminated Land

An initial view

During my working career, I and members of my environmental staff carried out many investigations of contaminated land. The purpose was to ascertain how badly it had been damaged, the nature of the contamination and what needed to be done to bring it back to use.

There was one major site in Fulham, West London, on which we were employed to carry out a major investigation. Our principals were the people who wanted to buy the site and the major construction firm, who would carry out the work.

The site was an area overlooking the river Thames. Once developed, the site would not be short of buyers wanting to live there and was destined to become a prime site. It consisted of a series of holding tanks close to the river for easy access. The site was bombed by the Luftwaffe in 1941 and one of the tanks was set on fire, allowing fuel to flow around the area. Once the fire was out, the remains of the tank was removed, the bomb crater filled and a replacement tank erected. Part of the site away from the river had been set aside for low-cost housing. For some reason, the prospective buyers did not require this area to receive a thorough investigation.

At the time of our arrival on site, all four tanks had been removed and the whole site was open ground. You could, however, smell a background of fuel oil as you walked round. I noticed immediately a complete absence of 'No Smoking' signs. I was told that, as the risk was slight, there was no need. The following day a worker was cutting up some steel pipes with an oxyacetylene torch. There was a loud bang and the operative was thrown about 10 feet in the air. Fortunately he was not badly hurt and he recovered. The next day there were 'No Smoking' signs everywhere.

We started our investigations by creating a number of trial pits and some boreholes around the site to assess the contamination. The soil down to about six feet was generally contaminated with hydrocarbons. Below that depth there was a thick layer of impermeable London clay. This layer had prevented soil below the clay layer from being contaminated. There were areas where buildings had existed and foundations had been dug to a deeper level. These areas had to be examined differently.

In the main area we got the contractors to construct two long trenches with sides angled to prevent collapse. Water in the contaminated layer above the clay drained laterally into these trenches. We employed pumps at each ends of the trenches, together with oil/water separators. Separated water was checked for residual oil contamination, and if clean, was sprayed on contaminated land to assist in this process.

Separated oil was put into holding tanks before being removed for disposal by a specialist contractor. Records of remaining oil in separated water were kept, amounting to about 100 parts per million and levels of separated oil were recorded. It was satisfying to see remaining oil in the water dropping with time.

The water company had told us that when the oil level was satisfactory, they would tell us when we could put the water down the drains. The oil collected in the special container increased slowly as expected. At the end of the process, separated water was dealt with by Thames Water.

One of the trenches

Council Accommodation

The container for separated oil, which had been filling nicely, was inspected and found to be empty. I thought the relevant firm dealing with the oil had collected it and removed it from site. I was shocked to be told by the operative in charge that he had thought it would be easier put it in the Thames.

Next day, there were questions asked in the House of Commons about the oil sick passing the Palace of Westminster. The Minister in Charge of looking after the environment told members of Parliament that the culprit would be found and suitably dealt with. By the time plans were put into place to find the culprit, the river was past high tide and the water flowing out to the North Sea. Before anyone could investigate, all contamination had gone.

On one of my visits to the site, the company's Health and Safety (H and S) manager was present. I was having an interesting talk with him when his phone rang. It was from the Oxford graduate he had recently employed to do similar work on a site in Bath. The young graduate said, 'Great news Alf, we have found a Roman pavement.' He was then asked by Alf if he had a JCB on site? 'I don't know,' he replied. As instructed, he went to have a look. 'Yes, we have.'

His instruction from the H and S officer was, 'I want you to use it to destroy the pavement and call me back when you have done it.'

'But Alf,' protested the young man, 'this could be valuable.'

'Call me back when you have done it,' came the firm reply. 'Your job is on the line if you refuse.'

On another occasion I was told that the Fulham site had been closed down by H and S. The contractors had managed to knock over one of the tower cranes. Fortunately, it had fallen against a partly constructed building and the crane driver escaped unhurt.

Once it was clear that the main part of the site was safe, construction of the blocks facing the Thames was able to go ahead. After completion, we were asked to carry out a similar operation on the neighbouring site, which had been used for a gas works. There were no immediate plans for development, but the nature and degree of contamination would affect the site's value.

Further east you come to the site of Chelsea Harbour. This site had been active for shipping out fruit and vegetables grown mainly in Fulham. The coming of the railways had put an end to using the harbour for that purpose and it had gradually disappeared from view due to fly tipping and disposal of a range of waste products. Our first job was to find the harbour. After removable of surface rubbish, the sides of the harbour basin were exposed. Once the harbour had been emptied we were surprised to see that it was in a relatively good condition. It had been well constructed.

Chelsea Harbour

It was a painstaking job of disposing of the rubbish. Fortunately we did not find any special wastes which would require disposal to a licensed site under controlled conditions. We continued to work on the site of the dock area and surrounding areas. It took a few years to complete the development, which included a boating marina, a first-class hotel, flats, houses and a range of expensive shops. The tower building is topped by two or four penthouses. It was rumoured that Michael Caine was interested in buying one.

We also carried out a site investigation on the south bank of the Thames. Before conducting such a study, it is necessary to contact suppliers of services to the area, including water, sewage, electricity, gas and telephone. I contacted all necessary suppliers and the local authorities in the area, so that we would not hit any of them when digging our trial pits. I indicated on a map where we intended digging the pits, six in all. These would be dug by JCB digger, all well away from services.

The Thames Barrier

I did not take part in the site work, but one evening while listening to the BBC news I was horrified to hear that most of South East London was without electric power. Apparently there had been damage done to one supply box in the area we were investigating and this had triggered other supply boxes.

Without any discussion with me, the manager running the construction of the new buildings had decided to move one of our intended trial pits to a different area to make it easier for JCB access.

The JCB's bucket had hit the main electrical supply to the area causing others along the line to trip. There was a load explosion and flame shot into the air. Fortunately, JCBs are double insulated for such situations so the driver was perfectly safe. At the time we had one of our environmental specialists on site to log the trial pits. Our chap was holding his notebook near the trip pit. Although he was unhurt, his notebook was badly burnt.

In the enquiry that followed, I was able to show my original map of where we required trial pits to be located – and another map of where the offending trial pit had been dug.

19.

Visiting the Voelckers

John, Susan, my Mother, Fred

I found I had some Voelcker relatives living in Natal, South Africa. My father told me about them but we had never met. My father's cousin John had been sent to Johannesburg in the 1920s to set up Imperial Chemical Industries South Africa. He was not a scientist like many of the family, but an accountant. He built up ICI South Africa and lived in Johannesburg in a large site with a big garden. He became one of the richest people in South Africa and was friendly with people like Harry Oppenheimer, grandson of Sir Ernest Oppenheimer. A businessman and philanthropist, Harry Oppenheimer was educated at Charterhouse and Oxford. He was one of South Africa's foremost industrialists and a great friend of Britain.

John Voelcker then expanded his business concerns, becoming a director of African Explosives, de Beers diamonds, Anglo American and of some of the goldmines. On reaching the age of 60, he retired and bought an estate in Natal, near the Midmar Dam and Ladysmith, where he built a palatial house. He had a younger brother, Emile Frederick, known as Fred, and a younger sister called Susan. Fred spent most of his working life in the Dutch East Indies and was fluent in Dutch, while Susan worked in a hospital in Surrey as an almoner and was unmarried.

Hebron Haven

John invited Fred and Susan to join him in Natal where they both built houses on their brother's estate and both outlived him. Fred devoted his life to creating an arboretum, importing trees from many parts of the world, while Susan devoted her time to improving the lot of the bantus (black South Africans) and ran a school for African children.

When I was in South Africa, my mother flew out for a visit. After a short stay in Johannesburg we went to Natal, where we had arranged to meet our relatives. My brother John joined us on his way back from Australia.

When we arrived for our family visit, Fred was standing outside the house, looking just like my father in appearance and in the way he was standing. That is where the similarity ends. We stayed in a local hotel called the Hebron Haven, which Fred had booked for us. He said that we were lucky he had been able to get a booking as the hotel was very popular. He was friendly with the owner, he said, who had arranged to accommodate us. When we arrived we were the only people in the hotel. We realised that Fred was not to be believed – on this matter or any other. Fred seemed to live in another universe and most of what he told us was fiction.

Despite Fred's fabrications, we did manage to learn more about our family from other sources. John Voelcker had devoted his life to ornithology and spent much of his time watching and photographing bird life, especially on the Midmar Dam. John's second wife had a daughter, Lucinda, who, in 1979, married a William Barlow, the son of well-known South African businessman and cricketer Punch Barlow. William was also a very successful businessman and entrepreneur. William and Lucinda should never have married as their interests were so different and their marriage lasted only a matter of months. Lucinda then married an English Baronet, Sir Richard Brooke and they settled in England.

During our visit to Natal, we went to the school Susan helped to run. The school was funded by donations from local firms and people. On this particular Sunday, we were attending the opening of a new bathroom building. The school master gave thanks for those people who, through their donation, had made this possible. 'We must thank the Lord for the shining latrines we now have,' he said. The children then sang a popular hymn, with Susan leading the singing. Everyone was very pleased with what Susan had achieved for the school.

After our stay in Natal, we then proceeded north to Swaziland. The country is landlocked by Mozambique and South Africa and is an absolute monarchy. The land consists of hot high ground and cooler low ground, which supports farming. Despite its small population, it has the highest HIV prevalence in world, with an estimated 20 per cent of the population affected. In 2021 riots broke out by students wanting democracy and many people died in the fighting.

We had booked in to the Swazi Palace Hotel which was unique for allowing gambling to be available on site. My mother had never seen a fruit machine before so we showed her how to use it. She tried it and it started issuing money, much of it spilling on the floor. She did not realise it, but she had made £100.

That evening we went to bed, leaving our shoes outside our doors for cleaning. There was then a power cut that left the whole building in darkness. After an hour the lights came back on again. I went outside to see if my shoes had been cleaned. All shoes had gone. I thought they would be back again in the morning. Unfortunately they had all been stolen.

We then drove South to Lesotho (formerly Basutoland), which was quite different from neighbouring countries. They had distinctive hats and rode horses, the only people in Southern Africa to do so. The country's wealth is boosted by its three dams, constructed on three rivers, which supply Johannesburg with all its electricity.

When it gained independence from Britain, Lesotho was left with all necessary equipment to construct houses and maintain roads. This included Land Rovers, trucks, road rollers and JCBs. Within six months all had disappeared. The Colonial Office in London was keeping a watching brief over this young country and it was discovered that the Land Rovers, trucks and vans had all found their way to ministers' gardens. No maintenance work had been done.

We then went North again to the Kruger National Park. The Kruger is famous as being South Africa's biggest and best game reserve. But in my view it is not the best, not least because they have tarred over most of the roads in the park, which takes away the natural look.

We drove around for some time and my mother was getting bored. She wanted to know the feeding times in the park. I pointed out that this was not a zoo and animals had to hunt other species to survive. At that point she lost interest. She wanted to leave the park and find a gin and tonic.

After Kruger we drove north towards the Limpopo River and the border town of Messina (now Musina). On the South African side of the border post, the white officials were curt and unsmiling. Crossing over the Limpopo into Rhodesia at Beit Bridge, we were met by smiling, friendly officials, both black and white, who welcomed us to Rhodesia and asked us whether we had had a good trip. We then headed for Bulawayo where we would be staying for a while.

20.

A Passion for the Piste

Beginner's class

Since I was a small boy, I had always been interested in downhill snow skiing. I had watched it on TV, but realised that the opportunity to take part was not likely to happen for some time. As a family we rarely took holidays abroad, so the idea of snow skiing was not likely. My elder brother had gone skiing in Obergurgl, Austria, when he was about 19, but he disliked it and never went again.

Every year, Oxford and Cambridge universities took a party of about 450 people to ski just before Christmas. To balance up numbers, nurses from hospitals were included. The timing of the visit enabled them to take over a whole village before the season started.

I said I wanted 5ft 8in. The man said, 'Les Anglais' and shrugged his shoulders. His assistant started making clucking noises and said 'Poulet', meaning I was a chicken, ie scared. I went back two days later and exchanged my skis for two metre ones. The Frenchmen said, 'Bravo'.

My American Friend

The first trip I took, in 1958, was to Saas Fee, Switzerland. It was the time when you could not spend much money abroad and you were limited to £50 of foreign exchange. As a student, however, you could get a V-form which was worth about an extra £40. We travelled by ferry across the Channel, then by train in couchettes through France and Switzerland, then finally bus to the resort.

Saas Fee put on a tremendous holiday for us. Hotel accommodation, ski lift passes and tuition were included and the whole village arranged a party for us. As well as being incredibly lucky for us, it was useful from their point of view as they could make sure that all the facilities in the village were in good working order before the skiing season started. Our ski instructor had limited English. He kept shouting to us, 'Stand on the balls!'. I do not think he realised why we were all laughing.

Dressed up

Before the trip, I went to Lillywhites in Piccadilly, where they held pre-skiing classes in the evenings. Apart from learning the basics, I was also able to buy a pair of ski boots there. In those days, the boots were made of leather and consisted of an inner and outer boot. There was no support for the ankle and many of the injuries were the result of broken ankles. The modern boot is made of plastic and gives good support to about nine inches up from the ankle.

That first ski trip sparked an enduring passion. In all, I went skiing about 30 times over a 25-year period, becoming fairly proficient. Over that time, I skied in France, Switzerland, Austria, and Italy. My favourite place was France.

My first time in Val d'Isère, I went to hire some skis. Being 6ft 3in tall and not being a very proficient skier at the time, I ordered skis that were 5ft 8in long. The attendant said, 'Non, deux metres.'

The Sixth Man

Kandy who gave 'Fritz' his marching orders

On another occasion, we were planning a trip to Verbier but we were one short in our ski party. We had taken a chalet for six people and, there only being five of us, we needed the sixth person to avoid paying more money per person. So we all tried to find a third man to make up the numbers.

I was at a drinks party and met an American who said he was looking for a ski party to join. I took his details and he told me that he had not skied in Europe but in North America, particularly in Alaska. The other members had not been able to find anyone, so they agreed that we should let him join us. In any case, he only wanted to come for a week,

At that time we were all hard up, so we decided to do the trip on the cheap. Our economy measures meant travelling by coach from central London to Verbier in

Switzerland. During the outward journey our new colleague produced a bottle of champagne and glasses, which we thought was very kind of him. He told us about his skiing and all the mountains he had conquered. We all thought he was going to be a lot better than the rest of us. The journey out was one of the worst I have ever made, taking over 24 hours, with three changes of drivers.

When we finally arrived we found our accommodation. It consisted of three double bedrooms, which meant I had to share with the American. Not only did he snore, but he also walked in his sleep. In the middle of the night he opened the window, still asleep, and broke off an icicle about a metre in length. Then he walked round the room holding the icicle above his head. I led him back to bed and threw the icicle out of the window. I went to the kitchen, got a broom, opened the window and broke off every icicle in reach. I thought he might stab me with one in his sleep.

Next day we got kitted up for skiing and proceeded to the slopes. Despite his nocturnal adventures, he appeared normal in the morning. We took a ski lift up to the top of a mountain and set off down. He stood at the top, frozen to the spot and shouting, 'Wait for me!'. He had no idea how to ski. Despite all his chat, I did not think he had been on skis before.

After about 30 minutes of waiting for him to get going, we started skiing and said, 'See you at the bottom'. I don't know how he made it down to the bottom, I presumed he had walked down. Next day he didn't come with us. We saw him at lunch and he said he had a good morning's skiing but that was enough. We never saw him on skis after that first morning.

He kept a cigarette lighter, with which he kept playing. There was a dummy fireplace in the flat that he wanted to light. I pointed out that it was a dummy and had no chimney. He obviously took no notice of me. The next day after skiing, we came back to find the flat full of smoke and the fire alarm ringing.

One evening we went out to dinner at the Farm Club, which was holding a Mardi Gras party. There were decorations hanging from the ceiling. Our American friend kept flicking his lighter, he said to see whether the decorations were flammable. This was a rather needless experiment since the decorations were made of paper.

Suddenly, a sheet of flame shot up towards the ceiling, setting fire to the decorations. Everyone was ordered to leave while the fire was put out. As a result of the fire, the Farm Club was closed for cleaning and repainting. We all were lucky that we were not presented with a bill for redecorating and loss of business. Unsurprisingly, we were all banned from visiting the Farm Club again.

In the morning I told the American he was no longer welcome and should go home. He agreed. He would go back to America, he said, where the skiing was far better. We were all relieved to see him go. We all came to the conclusion that he had psychotic problems.

A friend of mine who could only do the second week arrived. It was nice to have a roommate who was normal and I could have a good night's sleep without fear of nocturnal roaming.

Our ski passes worked on all the ski runs except Mont Fort, for which you had to pay extra. Two of us decided to have a go at the mighty peak. We took the bubble up to the top station and noticed there were plaques with the names of the people who had been killed on the slope. I pointed out there were still a few spaces left.

We set off and it was immediately apparent that it was very icy. My friend, who was a better skier than me, led the way. I followed, but after a few turns, I lost a ski. I tried to climb up to it, but it was too icy. I thought I could do better by climbing up using the still-attached ski. I tried to put on the lost ski but I lost my balance and also the remaining ski. To my horror I set off down the slope, head first and turning over and over, with no skis to help me slow down or stop.

There was a crevasse halfway down the slope, running across the piste and surrounded by orange marker flags. I fortunately bounced over the crevasse, ending up with the orange flags around my foot. If I had fallen into the crevasse that would have been the end of me. It would have been me who occupied one of the unused plaques at the top station.

Beyond that point, it was a slow walk down to the bottom. My friend, who had arrived there by good skiing, was waiting for me. We had a drink in the bistro. It then dawned on me that the only way back to our chalet was to take a T-bar (shaped like a T to transport two people up the hill). I was feeling decidedly wobbly but knew I had to do it. There was no alternative. With the help of my friend I made it to the top. Fortunately it was the relative security of chair lifts after that.

When I got back to our chalet I was in a terrible state, shaking and deciding not to ski again. There was a knock on the chalet door and an Australian came in. He was a ski bum. These are foreigners, mainly Australian, who work illegally as instructors. Local instructors hate them for stealing their trade, under-cutting them and not having had safety training. Fights sometimes break out between the two groups.

He said he had seen me fall and that I could have been killed. He told me that he would sort me out and help me get my nerve and enthusiasm back. He would come to the chalet in the evening to be paid. You should never be seen paying a ski bum money. If caught accepting cash, they could be banned from the whole resort. Payment made, he arrived the following morning.

He set off at quite a pace and told me to just keep up. I did my best, but he quickly was far ahead of me. I then forgot my problems and slowly got my nerve back. I must say I have done Mont Fort twice since then without any problems. On both occasions it was good snow with no ice.

The Author jumping off a button lift.

Swiss Skinny Dipping

One another occasion I went to one of the largest ski resorts in Switzerland and, after a good day's skiing, we decided to go to a health club in the town. We started by going to saunas, separated into male and female. We then went to the swimming pool.

You could only use the pool if you were naked. We all stripped off and entered the pool. One third of it was indoors and two thirds in the open air. The pool was covered by a layer of ping pong balls to keep the heat in. The water was warm but the outside air was extremely cold. There was a Frenchman there who kept climbing up the ladder and diving in. He was well built and well endowed and clearly enjoyed showing off his physique.

Because the air was so cold, I swam underwater occasionally to warm up. One side of the pool consisted of a large picture window. Through the window was a bar and we were providing the cabaret for the people on the floor below. The following evening we went to the bar and watched the swimmers, all naked and unaware that they could be seen. I still have one of the ping pong balls, which I secreted about my person and brought home as a souvenir.

Another time we decided to take the bus from St Anton, where we were staying, to Lech further long the valley. Fortunately our ski passes worked in all the valleys in the Arlberg. We went to the main ski lift up the mountain and joined a very long slow-moving queue. Behind us there were many noisy young Germans. They were not going to queue but decided to walk over our skis to get to the front. Despite many in the queue shouting at them, they did not stop.

One of our party, an extrovert Australian girl called Kandy, struck the quick-release button on the back of one of the German's skis with her ski stick. As a result, he was left standing on one ski.

He stopped and we all pushed his ski to the back of the queue, with shouts of 'Go and join it Fritz!' His mates did not wait for him, but went on to the front and boarded the chair lift.

Next day, I thought I would wait until later when hopefully the queue would be less long than the day before. I only had to wait about five minutes to get on the chair lift. I had the lift to myself until, at the last moment, a young German joined me. It was the one who lost his ski the previous day. I looked at him but he just looked away. He was still fuming, and at the top he shouted something in German. I replied 'Ficken zee auf,!' which I think means f*** off. He got the message.

One afternoon we went to have tea at a hotel in Lech after a hard day's skiing. The tea room was very crowded but we found a table with six chairs. When the waiter passed by our table, he was pushing a trolley laden with delicious cakes and we asked the price. He said in perfect English, 'You could not afford them' and pushed the trolley to an area where many Germans were having tea. On the way back he said, on passing our table, 'Not for you, they are too expensive.' Many of the cakes had been consumed.

One of our party asked, 'Why are you so bloody arrogant?' The waiter replied, 'You think you can treat this place like Lyons Corner House. In any case you do not have the money. We in Germany do.' He said he had worked in Lyons Corner House in London where he had learned his English. 'Lyons is the sort of restaurant you are reduced to eat in,' he told us.

Since his German friends had eaten all the cakes, he went back to the kitchen to get some more. On the way back, a colleague stopped to talk to him so he parked his trolley near to our table. All of us got up and helped ourselves to the cakes, eating all of them. When he came back he found a completely empty trolley. 'You have eaten my cakes,' he said. We ignored him and talked loudly amongst ourselves. He then changed his attitude and said. 'I will now have to pay for the cakes. I know you have eaten them. I do not earn much money, there will be nothing left.'

One of our party pulled out a 10 shilling note (50p) rolled up into a ball and flicked it at him. He said 'Fritz, that is all you are worth. I hope you have learned your lesson.'

The Wall of Death

Fairly on in my skiing career I did the famously steep Wall at Avoriaz. A party of 12 of us were staying in a Swiss chalet very close to the French border. Fortunately, the ski pass covered all of La Porte de Soleil area of Switzerland and

France.

We skied over to Avoriaz, which was fairly easy and on the flat. We took the chair lift up to the town which was built on a rocky escarpment overlooking the whole area. We found a bistro and had a good lunch whilst keeping wine to a minimum.

Pit stop

After lunch it was time to return to our chalet. I looked over the escarpment and it looked incredibly steep. 'I am not skiing down there,' I thought to myself. Some of our party decided to take the chair lift down to the bottom. I decided to join them. When we approached the bottom station I realised I had never used a chair lift to descend before. At the bottom I waved the man aside and said I was going up again. At the top, I looked over the edge and saw with horror what I had let myself in for. The top part was extremely steep and narrowed like an inverted funnel with a very narrow piste down the middle. Either side consisted of rock. If you fell on these it would probably have been the end of you.

At the end of this top part you entered a mogul field. Moguls are created by skiers when they ski continuously over the same place thereby forcing snow into mounds. When well worn they look like inverted egg boxes. If you ski over the top of a mogul it is the quickest way to fall, so you have to ski over the sides, which usually saves you from falling but is incredibly tiring.

I negotiated the rocky bit by doing a series of short tacks down the narrow piste, travelling faster than I would have liked. It was then into the moguls. Once through that you were still not over the worst, but you finally then entered a wide area of easier skiing down to the bottom.

I could not see any of our party anywhere and assumed I was probably last down. I waited for a while and another turned up. It turned out that I was the first one down. I would never do it again, and realised why the locals call it the Wall of Death.

Zermatt

Early in my skiing career, the party I often skied with decided to go Zermatt. I had not been there before but I had heard much about it. Brian, the organiser, always left it to the last moment and booked for us to be away from Christmas Eve to New Year's Eve. This made it easy to get a good deal, since many skiers prefer to be there for New Year rather than Christmas. Hotels in Zermatt were offering good deals and we ended up being a party of eight.

The idea that it was in the shadow of the Matterhorn, the highest mountain in Europe, appealed greatly to me, together with the fact that cars were banned from the resort. Electric vehicles were provided to get you around. You can leave your car at the outskirts of the town and take the rack and pinion electric train into the centre. From the point of view of skiing, the slopes were not difficult but allowed you to go on long traverses. There are also mogul fields.

The population of 6,000 are mainly German speaking and Roman Catholic. A noticeable visitor was the Marquess of Queensbury who, apart from setting the rules for boxing, was the person responsible for Oscar Wilde's downfall and imprisonment.

Friends on the Piste

Christmas Day

21.

Full Steam to Bristol

About 10 years ago I saw advertised a special journey of the Bristolian, which would be steam hauled from Victoria station in London to Bristol. My brother David was also a steam fan, so we travelled together with a mutual friend. We decided to travel first class which would include a newspaper, morning coffee and lunch on the way and dinner on the return journey.

Whilst there was sufficient coal for the journey, water was a problem. In days gone by, steam locomotives picked up water from troughs between the lines by means of a scoop which was lowered beneath the tender. This meant that water supply was not a problem and trains did not have to stop to take it onboard. However, troughs disappeared when diesel and electric replaced steam. On our modern journey there and back, we had to rendezvous with water bowsers, provided by local water companies at three locations.

The train was pulled by a mainline Pacific locomotive. This has the wheel configuration of 4-6-2, indicating that the engine has four wheels in the leading pony truck, six driving wheels and two wheels under the driving cab. At the first stop, a small bowser was waiting for us with a hose, which would have been more suitable for watering the garden. The transfer of water took a long time and filled the tender to under half full. Another stop on the way was hastily arranged, which fortunately provided us with a full tank. This did, however, add to the time and we arrived late in Bristol.

We had Alan Pegler on board who provided us with an interesting running commentary. He was the man who saved the Flying Scotsman locomotive from the breaker's yard, buying it directly from British Railways in good condition.

An Example of a Pacific Locomotive

On arrival in Bristol there were two sightseeing alternatives. We could either go to a factory that produced Bristol Cream sherry, or see the Great Britain in its dry dock. We chose the Great Britain. The SS Great Britain was a remarkable ship. It was designed by Isambard Brunel to carry passengers and was completed in 1845. The ship had two ways of being driven. She had masts and sails to drive it by wind power and she was also driven by a steam engine and a propeller. She was able to cross the Atlantic Ocean in 14 days, which in those days was exceptional.

The ship was used to transport large amounts of immigrants to Australia. In 1885 she ended up in the Falkland Islands, to be used as a warehouse and for storing coal. She remained there as a wreck. Then, in 1970, a plan was drawn up to raise her up, make her watertight and tow her back to Britain. She was placed in the dry dock in Bristol where she was originally built. When we visited, much work had been done but there was still much more required to bring her back to her original splendour.

Our train trip back to London took far less time than the outward journey. We came back on the mainline Bristol to Paddington route. Private trains are not allowed to exceed 70 mph on the mainline. However, we had a high speed train (HST) in front of us and another HST behind us. We were not very popular as we were slowing up the whole timetable. We had to pull over to a siding on two occasions when we required more water. Some operators of steam specials on mainlines have two tenders behind the locomotive to reduce the number of water stops.

In the end, our driver was told to forget the 70 mph speed limit. Whilst we did not reach the same speed of the HST, we did exceed 90mph, which was well above its normal maximum speed on mainline excursions.

I thought Bristol was a very interesting city but I had not realised it had suffered so badly in the blitz. It was bombed repeatedly by the Luftwaffe, who were probably aiming at Filton aircraft building plant. Bristol's city centre was very badly destroyed and many people lost their lives. The damage was as bad as in the East end of London at the height of the London blitz.

SS Great Britain

22.

British Motor Industry

I have always been interested in motor cars, inspired, no doubt, by my father's interest. In my lifetime, his first car was an Invictor, which I scarcely remember. For some reason he did not like it, so it was sold and he bought a Wolseley 18/80 in 1938. It was a nice-looking car and one of its selling points was that it had an MG engine. The dashboard looked as if it had been designed with Art Deco in mind. You could always spot a Wolseley because all of their cars had a light on the front of the radiator, lighting up the brand name.

It had many advanced features, for example it had an automatic choke, two carburettors, syncro-mesh gears on second, third and four gears. It also had a feature I never understood. Below the front passenger seat was a trapdoor for jacking up the car. You could set it for one wheel, two front wheels, two back wheels, both front, or both back wheels. It seemed to me to be quite useless as you still had to get out of the car to change a wheel.

There was a blind over the rear window which the driver could operate from a lever above their window. When operated, you had no rear view. Being straight, it was possible to open the windscreen, which hinged from the top. The rear boot could not be opened from the outside so luggage had to be loaded by raising the back seat.

On the outside, the car had a foldable rack so that it could be extended to take suitcases held in place by leather straps. In many ways it was far in advance of its rivals.

The Wolseley

At school when my parents came to visit me I asked them to park out of sight from other parents who had more modern cars. Other boys would remark that the only two families with older cars were the Voelcker family and the Colville family. Commander Colville was the King's Press Secretary, so we were in good company. When watching news films in the cinema, I also noticed that Winston Churchill always used an open-top Wolseley when he was visiting places in WW2 and afterwards.

Finally, after having had two new engines and a rebore it was time for the car to be replaced. My father had bought it in 1938 and he replaced it in 1955 with the latest model Wolseley. My father was able to get some petrol coupons to allow him to drive during the war. He was involved in helping people to be fed through their own efforts and maintaining a balanced diet. The food ration was very meagre, people on average lost a stone in weight and it was rare to see a fat person. Heart problems disappeared. Perhaps we could learn from that today.

After the end of World War Two, when car firms had been producing army vehicles, it took some time for them to start producing cars for the home market. In some cases the models produced in 1939 were relaunched. It took about two years for new models to come onto the market.

I think the first of these was the Standard Vanguard. Although well designed and constructed, it was an extremely ugly car. After a few years the design was modified, which improved its looks.

Demand for new cars was so strong that, having placed an order and paid a deposit, the wait for delivery was a minimum of two years. There was also demand for cars for export. Secondhand cars could fetch much more than the cost price when new.

During my working career, on my first visits to South Africa, Australia and New Zealand and other Commonwealth countries, it was rare to see anything other than British cars. I find it very sad that foreign cars now dominate those markets. Despite the signs, the UK car industry suffered from political interference, appalling bad management and incessant strikes. It took someone the calibre of Margaret Thatcher to tackle the union problems. Unfortunately, by the time she was Prime Minister it was too late.

Standard Vanguard

The Ford motor company in Dagenham produced a popular small car called the Fiesta. Strike-ridden British Motor Company tried to compete and were planning to bring out a rival. At the time some workers were literally sleeping on the job, so newspapers suggested it should be called the Siesta.

By the 1960s foreign cars were starting to enter the UK market, despite the prevailing prejudice. It started with the French Dauphine, followed by the Germans selling the VW Beetle. We were then hit by Japanese cars. Initially they were poorly made and unreliable, but they were priced to undercut the competition. They soon overcame their problems and were better equipped than other makes on the market.

In the 1970s the last of the imports were from Russia. Their cars were very large and unsuitable for European markets. To counter this, they bought the production line for the Fiat 124 from Italy. I had one of these when working in South Africa. They were ideal being fast, reliable, and economical on fuel. In the UK it was probably cheapest small car on the market.

I needed a car for one of our salesmen and remembering how good the Fiat 124 had been, I bought one. As a car it was a total disaster. The firm producing them in Russia was called Lada and they put in their own Lada engine, which was slow and unreliable. They had also used Russian tyres which did not last long. In fact, there was nothing good about it. Although it was almost new, I lost money when I sold it because they had such a bad reputation. Imports to the UK eventually stopped due to little demand.

Meanwhile, imports of Japanese cars was fast growing, so Toyota, Nissan and Honda decided

to build assembly plants in the UK. I was involved in a very small way when the Honda plant was being built. Japanese inspectors were forensically examining every stage of construction. The firm building the plant was being driven mad by Japanese inspectors wanting every stage of construction checked for accuracy.

All steel work had to be coated with an anti-rust material, which had to be of a certain thickness. The inspectors had claimed that the thickness was insufficient and not up to standard. My job was to check the thickness at many points of the framework. I found it to be according to the specification and there was nothing wrong with it. The manager of the construction firm told me that he could not work under these conditions and would never again work for a Japanese customer.

Although we produce many cars in the UK, all are for foreign-owned companies. For many years Morgan Motors was the only British owner manufacturer. Two years ago Morgan was sold to an Italian company. Rolls Royce, Bentley, Aston Martin, Jaguar, Rover, MG, Land Rover, Mini Vauxhall, and Lotus are all foreign-owned. Ironically, this comes at a time when most Formula 1 racing cars are made in the UK.

Fiat 124

Lada 130

23.

A Career Change

In 1971 I returned to the UK from South Africa and started working again with P-E Consulting. I realised I had had enough of working for one of the big four managing consulting firms. I wanted to find a small firm that I could acquire and improve, ideally a firm that wasn't making a profit but had the potential to do so.

I looked at a number of firms, from stationers to wheelwrights, but none fitted the bill. Then I saw an advertisement in the Financial Times offering a freehold factory unit for sale, 'at present being used for making furniture'. This seemed interesting. It sounded as if the business was not succeeding financially. I arranged a visit and liked what I saw. So I did a business proposal and submitted it to the National Westminster Bank to raise enough money to purchase the business and provide some working capital. NatWest agreed to provide the money and I acquired the firm.

It was based in High Wycombe, known at that time as 'England's Furniture Town' and was producing a range of chairs and settees (see photos). It consisted of a double-storey factory building of 5,000 square feet and a two-storey house, which served as an office and also housed three seamstresses who sewed the chair covers.

The 30-strong staff had an average age of 64. We had four excellent foremen in charge of the mill, frame making, polishing and upholstery. All four were different but great characters who had been in the industry all their lives.

The first job was to look at the range of products they made. There were about 15 different models, mainly individual chairs with a few two-seater settees and the occasional rocker. Some of the models dated from the utility scheme of the war years. Upholstery fabrics were produced in the UK and Italy. Chair frames were constructed from beech imported from Yugoslavia. However, not one finished beech part was common to more than one model, which left room for improvement. Scope also existed for reducing the existing range by weeding out the slow movers and also introducing new designs.

Complete kits of cut beech parts were stored for each design, resulting in money being tied up unnecessarily in stock, as well as taking up floor space. This stock wasn't standardised. For example, side rails of similar dimensions, which joined the chair's front and back legs, should have fitted the majority of all models. However, although they were identical in length, the three holes into which the standard dowels were slotted, were at different spacings. This rendered them only suitable for one model. After standardising the hole configuration, we were able to make the chair rails common to all models.

Although all our machinery was old it was possible to make further improvements by changing the methods of working. For example, straight rails were put through the planer one at a time, which was not time efficient. To speed things up, we could put them through twice or three times the length and then cut them to size. Each chair part was examined in the same way to see if production could be standardised between models. In all, reducing wooden work-in-progress in this way resulted in stock being reduced by 40 per cent and therefore also greatly reduced the money tied up in it.

My brother John joined me in this venture and was mainly in charge of sales. Some of our chairs were similar to Parker Knoll's (PK) range. However, we were producing 150 chairs per week, whilst PK produced about 4,000 chairs in the same amount of time. In the early 1970s when we started, new house building in the UK was at its height. Furniture sales followed house building closely because consumers tend to buy furniture when they move house.

Wing Chair

Fireside Chair

Gainsborough Chair

Bedroom Chair

PK were quoting 16 to 20 weeks' delivery, whilst we were quoting two to three weeks. Our products were about one third cheaper than theirs, but the quality was just as good. Hence there was scope for us to increase sales, as long as we could increase production.

However, in the early 1970s unemployment was at its lowest in the UK, being about 600,000. Many of these were unemployable and hence it was difficult to take on suitable staff, although we would provide them with training. This shortage of skilled staff held back our sales.

In 1974, the miners went on strike for higher pay. The Prime Minister, Edward Heath, introduced a three-day week in order to conserve electricity. Once this was over, the Trucial States around the Arabian Gulf, having been given their independence by Heath, realised along with Saudi Arabia that they could control the supply of crude oil to much of the world. As a consequence, inflation soared, reaching 28 per cent in the UK by the late 1970s.

The first industry to collapse was house building, followed, inevitably, by the furniture industry.

In response to the lower consumer demand, PK cut their prices by one third and offered almost immediate delivery. We could not profitably compete with this. Their prices were now similar to ours and therefore we had to cut our prices, which left us no profit from our products.

I tried to predict when the furniture industry would be likely to pick up. It seemed to me that this would not happen until the first half of the 1980s. In fact, it turned out to be a lot later. When it did, flat-pack furniture, pine furniture and Scandinavian design had arrived. We also saw the arrival of the discount furniture warehouses. One man who operated discount warehouses in the Midlands said he would take 1,400 chairs a week off us if the price was right. Our production amounted to 150 units per week, so we did not pursue this approach. We did look at the export market but could not find any takers.

It got to the stage when we were having to increase our bank loan from Nat West to pay our monthly loan instalments. I talked to our bank manager and we agreed that the only solution was to put the company up for sale. It took six months to find a buyer. Fortunately, when we bought the firm it included the freehold property and this enabled us to make a modest profit. The buyer was in the furniture business, so thankfully the staff kept their jobs.

My brother John took it hard and was very sorry to see the firm go. However, we had no choice and luckily the timing was right. I think we were the first of the small firms in High Wycombe to decide to sell. We did it at the right time. Many followed and it was no longer 'England's Furniture Town'.

As the bank manager pointed out, many struggling firms try to borrow more money to keep them going. In most cases, the firms were already too far gone to save themselves. Losing a business you have worked so hard to build is certainly very hard. During our time in business, when things were hard, two firms were destroyed by fire in dubious circumstances. Over a 12-year period, the number of furniture firms in High Wycombe went from about 300 down to one – and that was in the hands of receivers.

Our time in the furniture industry proved to be a very interesting exercise but it did not make us much money. However, I found it a pleasant undertaking and enjoyed having a tangible end product, rather than being a consultant producing paper reports and advice that some people did not want to follow.

Some of my consulting assignments were due to demands from shareholders for better returns, from the workforce for better pay, or to fend off a takeover. In two assignments I carried out, the problem was the chief executive. We advised that he should be given garden leave and a younger, more dynamic person found to replace him. An injection of forward-thinking, modern approaches certainly was necessary in the furniture industry, despite the decline in the furniture market.

In all, it had been a useful and interesting venture, but the timing was wrong. Also, we were making a quality, classic product when we should have introduced more up-to-date designs. But my experience didn't go to waste. The knowledge I had gained about chair making was sufficient for me to win an assignment later to help plan a chair-making.

Frames waiting to be upholstered

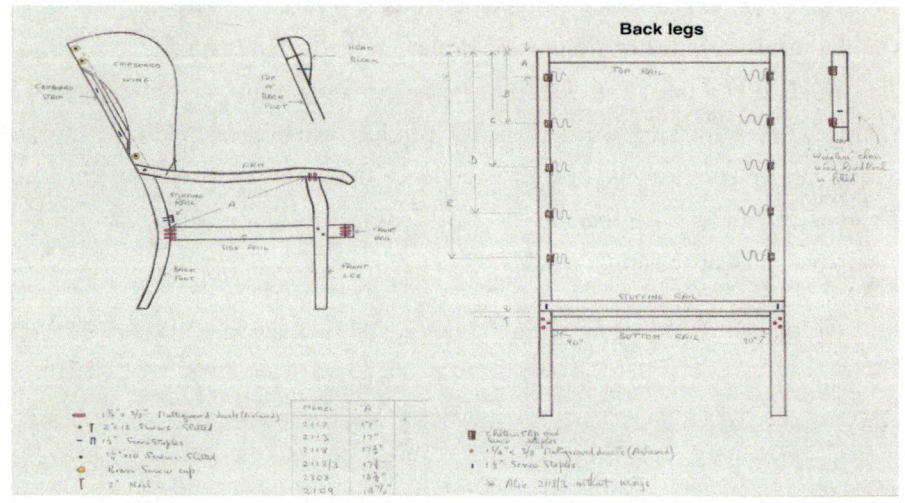

Sketches

24.

Egypt

During my working career I visited Egypt many times and always enjoyed my time there. My first visit was on my way back from an assignment on oil tankers in the Arabian Gulf. My next visit to Cairo was as part of a Department of Trade and Industry (DTI) trade mission to Egypt arranged by The British Consultants Bureau (BCB).

The BCB was set up to sell the services of British consultants to overseas firms in need of help. Consulting services were largely from engineering firms but there was a long tail of other companies, including ourselves. The BCB was a very successful enterprise and accounted for selling £3 billion of work per year to overseas firms. Its patron was the Duke of Gloucester.

About 250 of us flew to Cairo in a specially chartered BA plane. We were put up in two hotels, in my case the Conrad Hotel. We had to forward our promotional literature in advance to the Egyptian organisers. Local firms could indicate whom they would like to meet.

The meeting was housed in a large building, each firm with its own work station. It was well organised and it was spread over two days. I had about 15 representatives from firms who wanted to meet me. I had recently sold my practice to one of the privatised water companies. I told them that if they gave me some of their literature I could sell for them as well.

I had a chance to ask some of the older delegates what they thought of the way Egypt was governed. No one was enthusiastic. They said it was much better under King Farouk. They could forgive him for his string of lady friends and he had the knack of choosing competent people to run the country. The people running the country after Farouk were incompetent and corrupt.

After two days in Cairo, we took the train to Alexandria and repeated the exercise. The train looked like an electric unit but was, in fact, driven by steam. What looked like the first carriage was actually the steam locomotive.

Having lived through World War Two, it was interesting to visit a place I had heard about. We visited a number of pubs in Alexandria and most of us asked for an ice-cold beer, having remembered the film 'Ice Cold in Alex'.

We were given a drinks party by the British Ambassador at the Embassy. On taking up residence in an embassy, the ambassador can choose from paintings kept in store in the UK to adorn their new home. Apart from having a pleasant evening, I was very pleased to see a number of original David Roberts paintings. He was a theatrical stage designer, but his hobby was to visit Egypt and the Holy Land in the 1830s, when he would produce magnificent paintings. Our evening entertainment consisted of an excellent dinner on a boat on the Nile, with various cabaret acts including whirling dervishes and a belly dancer.

On another evening we had a trip to the Pyramids and a Son et Lumière performance. We travelled in two buses with an armed army escort at the front and another at the rear. There had recently been attacks on foreign tourists and the authorities did not want us to get into any trouble.

Unfortunately, the leading escort truck did not take the turning off the main road to Giza. There was confusion once their mistake was noticed. We all had to back beyond the turn off and start again. We were lucky: we would have been sitting ducks if anyone had wanted to attack us.

The leader of our party felt he should make a speech of thanks at every opportunity. Despite being corrected by members, he kept referring to the president of Egypt as Saddam Hussein, which did not go down well with our hosts. The president at the time was General Sadat. Apart from making speeches, our party leader's sole conversation to the locals was the Suez Crisis of 1956, which we found rather embarrassing and very tackless.

Cairo had grown in population by about 10 million people over a fairly short period of time. To counter this, four satellite towns had been set up in the desert and people were encouraged to move there and firms to set up there. Apart from being pleasant places to live and work, they were designed to be in garden settings and to keep pollution to a minimum.

The first factory we visited had a tall chimney which was belching out a large cloud of black smoke. Our guide asked the driver to park some distance from the factory. He then rushed to the building and within minutes the black smoke stopped, enabling us to enter.

We visited three factories in all. The first was a small rolling mill producing steel bars of varying thicknesses. The second packed tea into tea bags. The third produced cigarettes on rather ancient machinery. There were also a few British subsidiaries there. One made electric wiring webs for Land Rovers and another made top-end shirts under the name of Savile Row.

On another visit to Egypt, I visited a factory making carpets which employed child labour. Initially I was horrified. However, it was not quite as it seemed. Half the children made carpets in the morning and went to school in the afternoon. The other half went to school in the morning and made carpets in the afternoon. They all seemed very happy and looked well fed and well dressed. Child labour traditionally was common in the area, as it was for their parents but without the learning. I realised that in such areas, these children were the lucky ones.

As an agricultural scientist I was interested to see their method of farming. From above, one sees the river Nile with a green strip on both banks, then the desert as far as the eye can see. Every year the river floods, bringing fertiliser-rich silts which is a good growing medium for crops. I learned my lesson the hard way, by eating salad crops which had not been washed in clean water. The result was a gyppy tommy.

Before my visit I had sold our practice to one of the privatised water companies. It was one of the smaller ones which provided fresh water but did not handle sewage. They had a small consultancy section which did not seem to do anything. I suggested to our new principals that I could publicise their services as well as our own during my visit to Egypt. There was interest shown in the water company's work, as well as what we had to offer. On my return I gave the list of interested firms for them to follow up.

About six weeks later I received many letters and calls from Egyptian contacts to say that they had heard nothing from the water company. I telephoned to find out why nothing had been done. They said that they were busy working on their budgets for the coming year and were too busy to do anything else. I was furious and told them they were not capable of organising anything. I told them that, with this attitude, our consultancy had little future as part of their group. In fact, it took them just one year to destroy it.

Abu Simbul

On another visit to Egypt I went on a tour of the country, spending a week in Cairo, then took a flight to Luxor where we boarded a boat, the Sunbird IV, to sail up the Nile. It would normally take about 200 passengers. However, I had booked to travel two days after 9/11 when the twin towers in New York had been destroyed. About 100 passengers were American and they cancelled their trip in order to return home as soon as possible. Distressing as it was for them, I think that all of us remaining were rather relieved to have fewer people, as the boat's facilities, from bars, restaurants and the swimming pool, were never crowded.

We visited the temple of Karnak, which was well worth seeing. We sailed as far as the Aswan Low Dam and then up to the Aswan High Dam. The temple of Abu Simbel would have been submerged and destroyed by the building of the High Dam. President Nasser wanted the dam to be built to provide sufficient electricity for the growing population and expanding industrial sector.

The Abu Simbel temple was one of the finest relics along the Nile, being about 4,000 years old. A plan was drawn up to re-locate the site to higher ground. A competition was arranged for taking the buildings apart, which involved moving the parts to the new site and reconstructing it. The contract was awarded to a Norwegian firm who completed the job, and it is impossible to see any difference between the original building and as rebuilt. They certainly did an excellent job.

On the return journey we took an Arab dhow (boat) part of the way to Luxor. We then rejoined our boat for the return journey to Cairo. On our last night there was a party and we all had to dress up in Arab gear.

I already had my outfit. On my first journey to Abu Dhabi I had gone to the souk (market) and bought myself a Gulf Arab's outfit. This consisted of a dish dash, the white main garment, a turban and a black rope headpiece. I had fortunately taken my outfit on this trip in case there was an opportunity to wear it. I spent quite some time preparing for the party. I wanted to burn a wine bottle cork to give me black eyes. The barman was no help, as all his corks were plastic and therefore not usable. I then heard the sound of a champagne bottle being opened. I knocked on the cabin door and obtained its cork.

Back in my cabin I burnt the cork and gave myself a black moustache, black eyes and cheeks. I then put on the outfit and my glasses. I joined a table with two men and two women. For those who, unlike me, did not have an outfit to hand, our guide led a trip to an open-air market to buy material for them to make their own, or to improvise.

Arab Dhow

Dinner on board

One man at our table (pictured in the middle of the photo) had been in the Royal Navy and served in World War Two on the battleship HMS Nelson. When he retired from the navy he thought he would take up teaching. Not having been trained, he could not be a teacher but had to be used as a teacher's assistant. He was very popular with the pupils and was eventually allowed to become a teacher. He was told that he could not use his naval rank of commander, or to talk about his wartime experiences. He was to be plain mister. He proved his worth by enabling his pupils to obtain good exam results and a few gained entrance to universities. I was sorry I did not keep up with him after the trip.

On an earlier visit to Cairo, Dr Billingham and I decided to examine the Great Pyramid at Giza more closely. In those days it was possible to enter and travel through narrow passages into the centre of the Great Pyramid. We got as far as Tutankhamun's tomb which was completely empty. The contents had been taken to the museum in Cairo. Many excavated tombs were also found to be empty, but their contents had been looted by tomb raiders. When somebody died their goods and chattels were buried with them. Raiders would find a tomb, loot the contents and sell them. Being inside the Great Pyramid was an unforgettable experience.

Our boat for travelling up the Nile

25.

Chatham Naval Dockyard

I first visited Chatham Naval Dockyard at the age of 14 when it was fully operational. A cousin of my mother was in command of it at the time and he lived in a fine Regency house nearby. An NCO was appointed to take myself and my younger brother John around the dockyard. We saw many well-known Royal Navy warships that were either docked or being refitted.

When we visited, two crews were competing to represent Chatham in the annual Royal Tournament at the Earl's Court Exhibition Centre in West London. The winner would compete with teams from other dockyards, including Portsmouth, Plymouth and the Fleet Air Arm. My mother's cousin, Morris Parry, was shouting encouragement to the two teams using rather fruity language.

The field gun competition involved Royal Navy teams competing to transport a field gun and its equipment through a series of obstacles in the shortest time. It was based on an event in the Second Boer War in 1899, when the British garrison Ladysmith was being besieged. The army was doing badly and the Royal Navy went to their aid by demounting guns from two ships and transported them inland by train and then by oxen. The guns were then transported across very difficult terrain, including a ravine, which the sailors negotiated while hanging on to wires carrying guns, wheels, and all other equipment required.

The Field Gun competition started in London in 1907 and continued apart for the war years until the Royal Tournament was discontinued in 1999. Before the First World War, the competition was moved to Whale Island where it continued to 1973.

My old school, Wellington, has maintained the spirit of the relief of Ladysmith by continuing this event annually, using pupils from the naval Section of the Combined Cadet Force. It has proved to be very popular.

During our visit to Chatham Naval Dockyard, the NCO (a non-commissioned officer) said we could make a 78 RPM record of our visit. My brother John started off by giving a description of the fine buildings we had seen. When it came to my turn, having always been interested in naval warships, I gave the names and description of ships currently in dock.

Field and Gun Competition

The record was immediately stopped because what I was saying was confidential information. I was very sorry, as I could not see any harm now World War Two had been over for four years. I do not know how I managed it, but the stopped record came home with me. I still have it.

Over the years Chatham has built many fine warships. The best known is HMS

Victory, a ship of 104 guns and a crew of 800. It was launched in 1765. It is well known for being Admiral Nelson's flagship at the Battle of Trafalgar in which he lost his life. After his death, it became the flagship of Admiral Jervis at the battle of Cape Saint Vincent off the south-western coast of Portugal.

I was very sorry when Chatham Naval Dockyard was decommissioned as the navy was being slimmed down after World War Two. It is now a museum, which I visited in 1980 with my brother David and his wife.

HMS Cavalier in Dry Dock

I was particularly interested in seeing HMS Cavalier, the only destroyer from World War Two that had survived. HMS Cavalier was a C class vessel built in 1944 by Samuel White in the Isle of Wight. It was one of 32 C class ships built. Although it is now 75 years old, its design evolved through the classes, starting with the Tribal class. It was the fastest ship of all the C classes, able to exceed 31 knots.

For a long time it had been left in Southampton, rusting away and threatened with the scrap heap. Various attempts had been made to try to save it, but none had been able to raise enough money. I had given up hope, so was delighted to see it in Chatham looking great.

Destroyer of Similar Design to Cavalier

Some of the buildings in the museum are new and are used to demonstrate the various stages of building a ship. I was particularly interested in the Mould Shop, which is the stage when a wooden template is converted into a part of a ship. I found it interesting that building a wooden warship uses some of the same techniques as those of the more modern steel ships today.

One of the sheds is now used to displaying RNLI Lifeboats. It was fascinating to see the development from open rowing boats, the historic Grace Darling lifeboat, to large modern ones with steel hulls, and smaller ones with rubber hulls.

The Lifeboat

26.

Currying Favour

Our company, Voelcker Science, operated with two sections. I ran the environmental section and in 1990 I was looking for a chemist to run our food section. I recruited Dr Jack Chudy, a well-qualified chemist with a doctorate from London University and a further higher qualification in chemistry that he had gained in Poland. After that he had worked for Cadbury Schweppes, ending up as the director of quality for soft drinks.

Jack was the ideal candidate for us because he had some much-needed experience, having worked for the Laboratory of the Chemist. However, I was not sure whether we were right for him. Ours was a small practice employing 25 people, whereas Schweppes was a much larger organisation.

I suggested that he sit in my office for three days so that he could listen to what I did and meet visiting clients. He also accompanied me on site work. After two days he said he was convinced and he joined us immediately to run our food section.

The timing could not have been better. The following day I was contacted by a client producing Indian sweets but who was keen to set up a plant producing Indian foods, principally curries. His name was Goulam Noon and he was an Indian Muslim who had been expelled from Uganda by Iddy Amin. First he went to the

USA, but this did not work for him so he decided to try London. He said he was horrified by the curries being produced in the UK. He saw his role as being that of a person who knew how to do it properly.

I went to visit Mr Noon the following day, taking Jack with me. He had rented a space in a building that had once been a bus depot but was now divided into eight units. It was really too small for what he wanted to do. Fortunately, the next door unit became available, which made his proposal more viable. His aim was to let the British people find out what real curry should taste like.

He succeeded in his aim. Based on this success, he added another, much larger, factory to increase production. By this time Sainsbury's was his largest customer so he got the deputy chief executive of Sainsbury's to open the new factory. In his opening speech, Mr Noon thanked Dr Chudy and me for our help. He said he could not have done it without us.

Mr Noon was knighted and later on became a life peer. Lord Noon eventually sold out to a large food manufacturer and was then able to concentrate on his great love – cricket – becoming a member of the Marylebone Cricket Club, the MCC. He spent part of his money in setting up facilities for the 'untouchables' in India, those regarded as the lowest of the low.

Taking on Coca-Cola

In the early 1990s, consulting scientists were not the test houses they would become later in the decade, when widespread takeovers of small independent practices led to the disappearance of many long-established 'household name' firms. In those days we would turn our hand to anything remotely connected to our areas of expertise, where we felt we could satisfy the client and make some money. So, although analysis of food samples was our 'bread and butter', we would also turn our hand to other compatible activities.

In May 1993 a book appeared: For God, Country and Coca-Cola: The Definitive History of the Great American Soft Drink and the Company That Makes It. This was the (definitely) unauthorised history of the Coca-Cola company and, within its pages, was the 'secret recipe' for the world-famous drink.

The Sunday Times newspaper took an interest in the story and turned to Dr Augustus Voelcker and Sons with the simple request – could we make the drink, based on the recipe in the book? The request came through on a Wednesday and, in true enterprising spirit, we did not immediately refuse: we said we needed help with sourcing some of the more unusual ingredients listed, such as coriander or citrus oils. The newspaper agreed and since we had some in-house expertise of the soft drinks industry, we felt we could make a go of it.

Sugar and phosphoric acid were the least of our problems and the necessary carbonation was available in carbonated mineral water: so, all that was needed was to make up a concentrate, dilute it with carbonated water and fill it into glass mineral water bottles. But the 'recipe' was a bit vague in places, with units of weight and volume of the ingredients not specified. Moreover, the Sunday Times was thinking of an answer in time for their next edition, so time was against us. Thursday morning saw all the ingredients in place and so during the day some intense 'trial and error' formulation activity was undertaken, all the time referring to samples of the 'real thing' for comparison. We were aware that some of the ingredients were in short supply so could not be wasted on failed prototypes: the pressure was not only in the bottles of fizzy water!

By Thursday evening we felt that we had got as close as we could, given the time constraints. Also, we were running short of some ingredients (there had been failures along the way). The Sunday Times was contacted and they hastily arranged a Friday taste panel of 10 'cola drinkers' who were asked to identify Coca-Cola from among six drinks anonymously presented to them. These included the genuine article, our drink (by now named Actonola by the Sunday Times) and four others, including supermarket own-brand colas.

It was a nerve-wracking time leading up to the presentation – what if the Actonola was so different that 10 people immediately identified it as some unpleasant mix of approximately the right colour, but with little else resembling Coca-Cola? To our great relief, it soon became obvious we had created something not too far removed from the real thing. Our success was confirmed when the testers were asked to pick the genuine Coca-Cola from the six drinks presented to them: two picked correctly, three chose Pepsi Cola – and three chose our Actonola!

So, in just one day we had come up with a drink very close to the established market leaders.

On Sunday, the newspaper published their story and we were identified as the creators of this copy cola. On the Monday, several newspapers printed stories about Actonola and during the day we were asked to provide someone to appear live on Sky News that evening. The studios were not far away in Osterley and they sent a car.

You wait in the wings (smelling of stale cigarette smoke in those days) until the appropriate commercial break, then you are ushered into the seat next to the presenters and asked questions about the work: no reruns, no editing out of mistakes and five minutes later you are back in the wings. It was the early evening news (before 6pm), so the whole country was definitely not watching. And so, we got our fees and some free publicity for the firm, for doing work we had never done before – or ever did subsequently.

Detecting danger

We were approached by a French local authority to investigate a site required for building an old folks' home. The site, which had previously been used for making transformers and electrical switch gear, had been empty for some time and it had been vandalised, with much of the copper and other metals stolen. Polychlorinated Byphenyls (PCBs), which are highly toxic, was used for insulation. When breaking off the metal, the PCBs were allowed to pour out on to the floor. In its current contaminated state, the site was not suitable for construction of the home. It required a specialist cleaner to come in and totally remove any traces of PCB before site preparation and building work could start. The use of PCBs is now being phased out due to their toxicity.

27.

On My Travels

Marble Boat   *the Long Corridor*

Duuring my first visit to China I had the opportunity of seeing some of the country and was able to capture many sights and experiences with my camera. We started off by being shown tourist locations in and around Beijing. We were first taken to the Summer Palace, which is where the Emperor used to retreat to in the summer. The Marble Boat and Long Corridor (pictured) were two of the places one had to see.

The reason for my visit was my employment as a consultant to the International Maritime Organisation (IMO), a UN agency based in London. The Chinese government had recently joined the United Nations and they wanted two consultants to take parties around Europe and the USA in order to teach their maritime experts about how the West deals with oil spills, containment and clean up. I was the European expert and Captain George Steinman was my American counterpart.

Part two of the assignment consisted of setting up a series of visits to companies and organisations in Europe for them to learn how the West deals with such problems. We then flew to Paris to start the tour and at the end of it I took my seven pupils back to Beijing.

An Extraordinary City

I lived in Australia for nine years and returned to London for the UK summer after spending the Australian summer in Brisbane. To make the return journey more bearable, I always broke it with a stopover for a few days. Most of the time I stopped in Singapore, which I came to know well. I also tried new cities I had never visited before, including Kuala Lumpur (KL) and Hong Kong.

I liked KL but, to me, it had the feeling of trying to be a second Singapore and not always succeeding. It was a pleasant city, but it did not have the levels of service and design you find in Singapore. For example, who would want a city airport situated about 70 miles from the city?

I stopped off in Hong Kong on two occasions for a few days and found an extraordinary city which I had never imagined. For example, the extreme difference of various levels of the population, from the well-off driving around in stretched Rolls Royces and other expensive cars, to the very poor begging in the gutter.

After World War Two, the tremendous influx of displaced and stateless emigrants resulted in a massive drive to build accommodation in Hong Kong. It resulted in a density of tall residential apartment buildings, constructed so close together that you could touch one building to another. Many seem to have permanent washing hanging out.

Hong Kong has a very turbulent history. In 1842, the Treaty of Nanjin ceded Hong Kong Island to the UK and ended the first opium war. After being occupied by the Japanese from 1921 to 1945, Hong Kong was returned to being a trading centre after the end of World War Two. Then, during the 1950s, industries were set up and manufacturing flourished.

In 1984 British Prime Minister Margaret Thatcher signed an agreement to return Hong Kong to China. This came into effect in 1997. The idea agreed was that Hong Kong would have elections and their own form of government based on the British system. But in 2003 the Chinese Government overruled the elected government of Hong Kong and tried to impose their own communist ideas, sparking mass protests

The Author on the Great Wall

Tiananmen Square

Aberdeen's Famous Floating Restaurant

Since then, Hong Kong people have been subjected to repeated pressure from Peking to obey edits covering China as a whole. Repeated attempts to overrule Hong Kong's own legislature have produced riots and mass disagreements. A firm hand from the police has produced many injuries and deaths, particularly among the young. Many people have been imprisoned and others have decided to relocate to the UK.

Turkey

Four of us decided to have a holiday in Turkey as none of us had been there before. One of our number, Colin, could be very moody, especially if he could not get his own way and I was not keen on allowing him to join us. He fell into a sulk even before we left the UK. Colin said he wanted to drive in his car down to Gatwick, but the rest of us were not in favour. We wanted to go by train to the airport, which we thought would be simplest and meant Colin would avoid parking problems. He insisted on driving, but we were adamant that we would be going by train. He fell in with our wishes reluctantly, saying we had forced him take the train.

Lorne, Colin, Debbie and Me

We flew from Gatwick to Daliman and then took a bus to Kalkan, where we were staying for the first week. It was a pleasant resort with good swimming and sailing, but with concrete beaches. There were, however, loungers for sunbathing. We had booked to spend the second week in Bodrum. This resort was mainly for package holiday makers and there were crowds everywhere you went. We decided to dine late as most tourists wanted to eat about six o'clock.

At our first dinner the waiter tried to talk to us in English. He was doing his best and we could just about understand. Colin then made fun of the waiter, so I told Colin to talk to him in Turkish. I was told I was being stupid.

By this time the two girls, Debbie and Lorne, who were friends, refused to talk to Colin. I had to share a room with him. That evening after dinner, he said I should be supporting him and that I should tell the girls they should join us in conversations. I pointed out that he was being a prat.

In the morning he said to me, 'You called me a prat last night.' By this time all three of us were regretting we had allowed him to join us.

On the second day in Bodrum we were joined by a friend of one of the girls. Mike was British but lived in Perth, Australia and was good company. He was on a pilgrimage to see the Australian cemetery at Gallipoli, where many thousands of Australian and New Zealand troops had been killed in World War One.

Winston Churchill, then First Lord of the Admiralty, had designed the Gallipoli campaign to defeat the Turks and shorten the war. Turkey was on the side of the Germans and he thought that by removing Turkey and taking control of the Turkish Straits, Germany would probably capitulate. However the British Parliament took a long time to debate the plan. By this time the Turks had found out about it and were ready to defend their country. After months of fighting, the plan was abandoned and the invading troops who had landed on the Gallipoli peninsula were withdrawn. There was a huge loss of life on both sides, including the sinking of two British battleships and one French. The Australians have never forgotten the disaster and to this day are resentful about it.

We decided to take a four-hour bus journey to Ephesus, which had been an important Roman settlement. Ephesus is reputed to be the burial place of the headless John the Baptist. The city came under control of the Roman Empire in 129 BC. The city was destroyed by the Goths in 263 and in 614 it was partly destroyed by an earthquake. It is now a UNESCO World Heritage Site. There are many sights to see. Probably the greatest is the Celsus Library, followed by the amphitheatre.

Colin had already booked four seats on the bus and when Mike said he would like to come, too, I booked a seat for him. Our group of four boarded the bus, with Mike expected to join us five minutes later. Colin said to the driver, 'That's four of us, so we can go'. I told the driver there was one more to come. Keen to get going without Mike, Colin said, 'No he has been taken ill and cannot join us.' Mike then arrived and the driver said, 'I thought you said he was ill'. I said he had made a specular recovery. Colin said to me, 'Tell him to get off, we do not want him.' I replied, 'I have a better idea, why don't you get off.' Mike was very good company and we were happy that he joined us. By contrast, Colin went into a sulk.

Celsus Library

Bodrum

27.

Perth and Locomotives

Pendennis Castle

I had been to Perth a few years ago when I wanted to see the West Coast of Australia. Perth had been the third largest city in the country until being overtaken by Brisbane. Freemantle, Perth's port was the first port of call for ships from Europe.

A year later a friend, Lavinia who was working for English Heritage had an interesting project to carry out. This was to liberate a steam locomotive from Australia and bring it back to England. The locomotive was the Pendennis Castle, It was one of 20 Castle Class Great Western Railway built in Swindon in 1924. It was numbered 4079. It had been well maintained during its working life.

After much work on full restoration has taken placed, at times interrupted by Covid-19, it is now completed.

After the end of World War 2 many countries in Western Europe had to decide what form of traction should be adopted for their railways. Many engines had been lost in the war or were in a poor condition by lack of maintenance.

Electric was the most favoured but was expensive. Some went with diesel as a stop gap before electrification could be afforded. In Britain the decision was taken to keep with steam. The decision was taken on the basis that we had plenty of coal and steam locomotives were cheap to build. The designer Riddles was given the task of designing a range of locomotives. In all about 800 were built. As a result UK was behind other countries in electrification.

With the end of steam in the mid 1960s locomotives and wagons across the country were sent to scrapyards for breaking up.

Dai Woodham owned a scrapyard in Barry South Wales and bought about 300 engines, tenders and other wagons for breaking up. Being a steam fan the wagons came first and then the tenders. At one point he was forced to keep the yard busy by scrapping 3 engines.

Anyone and private lines could buy engines from Dai for their scrap value. This was all very well to start with when the engines complete. But as time went on looting occurred. All pipework, brass, gauges even connecting rods disappeared. These intended for rebuilding for private lines went up in value as more and more parts would require replacing. However if the boiler, frames and wheels were in reasonable condition this would count for about half the value of engine.

A group of which I am a shareholder decided to buy one Battle of Britain (BOB) /West Country engine which had lost its tender. Although two names were used the classes were identical. After using all the BOB names they had to change to West Country names.

The engine we had bought was 257 Squadron. It was a Pacific class, wheel configuration 4. 6. 2, four bogies, six driving wheels and two under the cab. Our group now owns six locomotives, in working order or being worked on.

257 Squadron, Before

After

Acknowledgements

I would like to thank those who have helped me in writing this book. They include Ceri McKellar, a fellow author in South Africa and Liz Billingham, a former director of one of the large publishing house's subsidiaries. I would also like to thank my ex-business partner Jack Chudy and Aileen O'Brien my editor.

Thanks also go to my computer experts, Francesco Braun, Neil Mason, Christie Griffiths and Bob Gould. They completed the work with a skill far beyond I could not have done myself.

Printed in Great Britain
by Amazon

83579584R00119